Trans World Radio

Broadcasting the Gospel worldwide

UNHINDERED POWER

In appreciation of your support, interest, and prayers on behalf of Trans World Radio's worldwide broadcasting ministry, we want you to have a personal copy of *Unhindered Power*, an exciting book that reveals the marvelous working of God's saving power through international radio.

From Africa to Asia, South America to Europe, we want you to see firsthand how God is touching people's lives with the gospel message by means of radio. Forty true stories, based upon Briar Whitehead's research and personal travels, demonstrate the impact of Trans World Radio's broadcasts, as well as those of other international broadcasters such as FEBC and HCJB. Nearly 1,000 hours per week of programs, transmitted from TWR's seven strategically located sites, reach areas of the world in ways we cannot imagine. This book highlights those ways. It presents not only the excitement of international radio, but documents the effectiveness of this unique missionary tool. Please continue to pray for this ministry.

Dr. Paul E. Freed
President

E. Brandt Gustavson
Executive Vice President

UNHINDERED POWER

40 True Stories of God at Work Around the World through Christian Radio

by

BRIAR WHITEHEAD

MOODY PRESS

CHICAGO

© 1990 by
BRIAR WHITEHEAD

All rights reserved. No part of this book may be reproduced in any form without permission in writing from the publisher, except in the case of brief quotations embodied in critical articles or reviews.

All Scripture quotations, unless noted otherwise, are from *The Holy Bible: New International Version*. Copyright © 1973, 1977, 1984, International Bible Society. Used by permission of Zondervan Bible Publishers.

The use of selected references from various versions of the Bible in this publication does not necessarily imply publisher endorsement of the versions in their entirety.

ISBN: 0-8024-9067-0

1 2 3 4 5 6 7 8 Printing/LC/Year 95 94 93 92 91 90

Printed in the United States of America

To the One who had the idea first.
To Neil, my best friend and source of cash.
To the TWR staff at Monte Carlo,
where most of the long gestation took place—
with much love and respect.

CONTENTS

FOREWORD

From the human point of view, Christian radio is absurd.

You sit in a studio and speak into a microphone. Your invisible words are carried by invisible waves to listeners you cannot see. In fact, you are never really sure that *anybody* is listening.

The whole thing would be absurd *except for the promises of God.*

God told Jeremiah, "I am watching over My word to perform it" (Jeremiah 1:12, NASB*). And He said to Isaiah, "My word . . . shall not return to Me empty, without accomplishing what I desire, and without succeeding in the matter for which I sent it" (Isaiah 55:11, NASB).

That settles it for me! Christian radio is *not* absurd! Instead, it is part of God's ongoing miracle of transforming lives through the power of the gospel of Jesus Christ. *Christian radio works.*

Briar Whitehead is a gifted writer whose prose is a delight to read. You will find no melodrama or cheap sentimentalism in these pages. Instead, she shares with us the excitement of the kind of evangelism that leaps over walls, penetrates iron curtains, enters hospitals and prisons, and visits the neglected hovels of the earth, and all for one purpose: to bring to hopeless people the life-changing message of Jesus Christ.

* *New American Standard Bible.*

I trust that your reading of this book will encourage you to be a part of the worldwide miracle of evangelism, starting right where you are. God uses many workers and many different tools, and He can use you. Please let Him!

WARREN W. WIERSBE

PREFACE

One thing you realize as you wander around the world is that people are the same everywhere. The man in Japan or India or China is no different in essentials from the man in England, Russia, or Argentina. He still fights with his wife, cheats the authorities, gets mad at his neighbor, claws his way up the corporate or party ladder, and hates his boss. One might murder with a look or with words, the other with a knife. A woman in Venezuela and a woman in France both commit adultery, have quiet abortions, and develop alcohol dependency as they struggle with their guilt. A student in Germany, a leper in the Amazon, and an anonymous listener somewhere in Iran are on the point of taking their own lives because it's easier to die than it is to keep on living.

The other thing you realize is that there is an answer as universal as the problems. A Master Key can unlock all the doors human beings close against their consciences—whether they live in Europe, black Africa, tribal Amazonia, Siberia, or the Far East, whatever religion they practice or to whatever culture they belong. Jesus Christ has a way of getting behind the barriers built to keep Him out and going straight to the person behind them who is really yearning to meet Him—because meeting Jesus Christ means an end to every man's struggle against his worst self. A simple matter of saying, "I'm so sorry. Please make me different. I want to follow You now."

Radio is not only capable of being everywhere at once, it is also a very personal medium, able to reach behind locked doors right into a person's heart. And at any of those moments, in a car, a lounge, a kitchen, a sickbed, in the garden, in the jungle, we might find one of the people in the first paragraph struggling with his guilt, or a death wish, or an addiction. And alone, wherever he or she is, with no one watching, no one to sneer at him or laugh, he stops what he's doing, leans over, turns up the volume, and listens.

He would never go near a church, never let on to his best friend—at least not yet—that he listened to a religious broadcast, but in the quietness of his own heart the vital rendezvous takes place, and he comes away different. Letters from all over the globe to the radio offices say it daily in scores of different languages: "Something has happened to me! I heard your broadcast. I found Jesus Christ."

Nothing can keep out a radio wave. Where missionaries cannot go, radio can. By simply being a radio voice, one man can become a missionary to millions without going anywhere. And the listeners are everywhere, at every level of society, wherever a program is broadcast. Sometimes in remote areas whole villages or regions listen. No one knows the total figures, but from east to west, every twenty-four hours as the world spins through the night to a new day, millions tune in either accidentally or deliberately. Many will keep listening—some in spite of themselves.

Many who know little or nothing of Jesus Christ will begin to admire and love Him. Those to whom Jesus is just another god will find He quietly demands the ascendancy. Some who call themselves Christians will realize they have never really believed. Then the encounter and reconciliation takes place, first with God, then with neighbors and colleagues and enemies. And out of it all come better husbands, wives, sons, daughters, workers, bosses—better people; more integrity, honesty, kindness, patience, humility, reasonableness, faithfulness.

Programs encourage listeners to join a church. Where they can't, the radio often takes its place. Sometimes churches spring out of radio listening; the existence of thousands of these "radio-churches" is well documented. Certainly the networks see themselves as an arm of the church. Their transmitters are open to denominations and groups wanting to use any of their one hundred fifty-two radio languages or to add a few more. Trans World Radio (TWR), Far East Broadcasting Company Radio International (FEBC), Heralding Christ Jesus' Blessing (HCJB), and Eternal Love Winning Africa (ELWA), the major evangelical international radio broadcasters, have joined hands now to mount a major evangelistic offensive called *The World by 2000.* Of all the missionary organizations, they are the best equipped to do it. With a combined strength of millions of watts, hardly a spot on the globe today is outside the reach of their transmitters. And who today does not own a radio?

The stories in this book are only a drop in the ocean. For every story told a million others are not told—and not even known—and hour by hour more are being added. The psalmist could never have known how prophetic his lines were when he wrote them: "Their message goes out to all the world and is heard to the ends of the earth." A radio wave and a message! Only at the end of time will the earth reveal its uttermost parts, and a million transformed people will stand up and say that they heard the Word, that the Word was not wasted, and that the Word was Jesus Christ.

Part 1

Part 1

Your broadcasts showed me that my whole family was walking to eternal death as if we had blindfolds on. Finally we had to admit that the old Book, covered with dust and superseded by science and progress, is still true. . . .

TWR
Czechoslovakia

I used to hear stories about Jesus Christ, that He healed the sick, opened the eyes of the blind and sometimes raised the dead. To me they were fables. All of a sudden as I kept listening I discovered Jesus Christ, and the way became bright before me. He overwhelmed me. My life is changed. I can't wait for your programs.

TWR
Tunisia

Your programs are like refreshing water for those of us who thirst. You offer relief for me personally as I struggle with daily trials. After I have dropped the children off at school, I quickly turn the radio on and seek the guidance that God would have for me from His Word for that day.

WMBI, WMBI-FM
United States

You make hope spring up inside me. It's impossible to explain how I feel when I listen. You are talking about things I long for but have never seen—like love and mercy.

TWR
Turkey

A French woman, given a Trans World Radio broadcasting schedule, wasn't remotely interested. She dropped it in the car glove box and forgot about it. When her husband was taken seriously ill and not expected to live, she was desperate. As she sat in the car crying, rummaging inside the glove box for a handkerchief, the broadcasting schedule fell into her lap. Sniffling, she looked at it and saw that a broadcast was about to start. She tuned in, and as she listened she decided to follow Jesus Christ. The comfort she felt as she prayed was so real that she went straight away to tell her husband, who, incidentally, recovered.

TWR
France

I began listening to you many years ago and have shared faithfully about your ministry with the people at church. I know many are constant listeners. The labor of love and dedication that you perform is effective in ministering to all of us who listen to you.

WMBI, WMBI-FM
United States

I feel I am being changed, and even my friends and relatives tell me I am different. I picked you up accidentally, and your words struck me. Now my friends are listening, and at school we discuss your messages.

TWR
Syria

I heard you read my mother's letter over the radio and then talk to us from the Bible. I really didn't know that I was causing my mother so much anguish. I have asked her to forgive me, and I will never treat her that way again.

TWR
Brazil

1

STARTING AGAIN

March 1, 1979

Marianne Bohner is slim and attractive and happy with life. Otto is a good husband, and her two young girls are growing into bright, healthy children. Their brand new, spacious, modern home in Gerstetten, south Germany, is just what she has always wanted. Now her main goal in life is to raise the two girls to be happy, well-adjusted teen-agers and, one day, good wives and mothers.

Otto Bohner has the tall, rangy build of an outdoor man, and he is a practical one, too. He built much of the new house himself. He's very active, an achiever: sets his goals and works toward them, impatient of hindrances. He's a good father. His immediate aim is to finish the house, his more long-term ones to do a creditable job of raising the kids, to find job satisfaction, and to run his own life.

Late April 1979

Marianne Bohner suddenly jerks into consciousness. She is in a hospital bed in an unfamiliar room. She can barely move.

Marianne recalls: "I woke up in the hospital. My first questions were: Why am I here? What happened? I was so confused. They told me I'd been unconscious for *six weeks.*

"I had to slowly and painfully begin to live all over again —learning how to eat, drink, walk, and think."

"I couldn't stop thinking, *What would have happened if I'd died?*"

Otto adds: "They gave her a plate of cereal and a spoon. She didn't know what to do with it. She just put the spoon in the plate and stirred it round and round and round. . . ."

August 1986

Now, seven years after the accident, Marianne sits quietly in her chair, an attractive, soft-spoken woman with a warm, slow smile. Physically, nothing shows of the accident except barely visible scars on her left temple and throat, and you're not really sure if you see or only imagine the slight disorientation she says remains in her walk or the weakness on her left side.

Her speech is hesitant at times; she can suddenly forget the word on her tongue. But there is a deeper hesitation: her neurologist says the accident has left psychological scars and that a woman who loses so many faculties loses her self-esteem, too. Her recovery had jumped ahead when she began to believe that God had a purpose in the accident and that it wasn't just a blind stroke of fate, he says.

Otto, in blue jeans and sandals, his hair and beard tinged with gray, looks too long for the settee; his knees stick awkwardly up in front of him. "What I kind of learned," he said huskily, "is that when it's good in your life you don't need God, but when it gets hard, you do. Before, I just took everything for granted. I think I'm a lot closer to God."

The day that so changed Marianne's life, March 1, 1979, was bright and warm; one of the first real spring days after a cold, gray, German winter. The snow was melting by the roadside as Marianne dropped her two girls at school early in the afternoon. She was due for a back massage in nearby Heidenheim at 2:00 P.M., and as the white VW Variant pulled away from the curb she was already wondering how she could get back in time to pick up the kids at 4:00 P.M. In her mind she was also packing and preparing for her spa cure. She was too tired, and the doctor had prescribed a rest.

The sun was behind her as she approached the railway crossing at Gerstetten's rural fringe. The way ahead was clear, and she wasn't doing more than 35 mph when she began to accelerate slightly. The strong sun shone directly onto the stoplights, fading out the red signal, and there were no safety barriers.

The two-carriage goods-and-passenger train that ran four return journeys daily through the countryside wasn't doing more than 25 mph as it approached the Gerstetten crossing. The driver saw Marianne before she saw him. There was plenty of time for her to stop, and the driver had no reason to think she wouldn't, because the railway stoplights were flashing red.

Train and car collided in a screech of tearing metal at a combined speed of 50 mph, locking the driver's side into the carriage and crushing in the driver's door. As the train dragged the car twenty or thirty feet, Marianne's head bounced against the doorframe, and jagged metal cut deeply into her temple. But that injury was only superficial. The critical injury occurred as her brain thudded against the inside of her skull, knocking her unconscious. When the vehicle finally fell free and came to rest facing in the opposite direction, it was a write-off. On-lookers quickly pulled Marianne from the car and laid her on the grass. No bones were broken, and the injury didn't look serious except for the deep gash in the temple.

Otto was working at the window in the Heidenheim Post Office when the call came through at 2:45 P.M. At first he thought one of his friends was playing a callous practical joke. But it was the police, and they said that Marianne was dangerously ill in the Heidenheim Public Hospital.

His hands trembling, he dialed hospital admissions, and they confirmed she was critically ill and under intensive care. Otto assigned his duties to the next window, took the rest of the afternoon off, and drove like a madman to the hospital.

He couldn't believe it when he first saw her, tied to a bed with no side boards, bristling with tubes and life-support systems, and shaking violently. "If she survives," the doctors told him, "you can expect her to be permanently paralyzed down the left side."

Otto was a strong man. He believed in God, but also that a man could get along all right without Him. He'd got along all right without Him so far. But he returned home that night shattered, and his voice quivers as he says that to get himself through the first few days he prayed and read the Bible, something he'd never done before. For the first twenty-four hours he was unable to sleep at all. "I just about had a nervous breakdown. It was a terrible shock." His hopes only rose a tiny fraction when, after two days, Marianne stopped shaking. "That was when I began to think she would live," he says. "The shaking seemed to be part of the struggle to survive."

For ten days Marianne's life hung in the balance as, one after another, her organs gave up the struggle and it became a medical balancing act to keep her alive; treatment for one organ threatening to overwhelm another. For four weeks she was completely unconscious from pain. It was a long six weeks before the next hopeful sign, and Otto's eyes fill with tears as he remembers the first time she recognized him.

Marianne recalls a few rare trips to the surface of consciousness between the fourth and sixth weeks. She remembers apologizing to a nurse because the bed was wet and she couldn't help it. Another time she seemed to be in a very narrow room with close, high walls, and she thought how strange it was. She did recognize her sister once, clearly enough to indicate it to her before she lapsed back into unconsciousness. But the sister she had seen was the sister of her childhood, and they were in the garden at home, playing together.

But this was the sign Otto had been waiting six weeks to see, and the following day she recognized him, too. His visit is Marianne's first clear recollection. "Where am I?" she asked him. "What am I doing here?" And the long painful rehabilitation started.

"What season of the year is it?" the doctor would ask. But Marianne couldn't remember what "season" meant. "Where are you?" he would say. "At school," she would answer.

Often people couldn't make heads or tails of her speech. But Otto could. "It was very slow with long pauses," he says. "Verbally she was about seven years old. And she had to be told things over and over again, because she couldn't remember them."

The therapists taught her how to walk again, round and round a big table, holding on to it. When she graduated to a straight, level path, she kept getting dizzy and falling over, and often wondered if she would ever walk normally again. They re-taught her basic arithmetic: how to count using brightly colored cubes. She made houses out of blocks. When she first began to read, she held the book upside-down, and even as she improved she still had to read everything twice before it sank in.

As she recovered, one question posed itself constantly: "Where would I be if I'd died?"

When she was a child her parents thought it was socially useful for one member of the family to go to church each month, and Marianne had been baptized, confirmed, and married in the church. Basically religion was irrelevant, though she had tried to live a good life. But when Otto drove her home for the first time, she was almost overwhelmed by the beauty of the landscape. "I suddenly thought, *If God made all this, I want to get to know Him,*" she says.

Transferred to another neurological clinic six months after the accident, she began going to the chapel looking for answers, but nothing she heard made any sense. One day at lunch, how-ever, a woman said to her: "Do you know about 'Evangeliums Rundfunk?'"*

"About what?" Marianne said. The woman repeated her-self, then explained. "I'll give you a program schedule." So Mari-anne began listening to the evening radio broadcasts, though they were often beyond her. "But I had to listen," she says. "It was almost a compulsion. Even though I couldn't understand a lot of it, I soaked it up."

* Trans World Radio's West German partner.

"Why do you keep listening if you don't understand it?" Otto said one day. "Turn it off." And after about three months, she began to think she probably should. God couldn't hold her responsible for something she didn't know. Anyway, how could she be sure that what she was hearing was true? "But I couldn't turn it off," she says. "And I didn't want to forget what I had already heard."

She started tuning in the early afternoon broadcasts as well and began to see that they were talking about a way of thinking and living that was totally foreign to her. "I began to see that I had to do a complete about-turn," she says. "This way of thinking was so different."

She mentions some of the programs that meant so much to her over the period. One was about the prodigal son who had taken his inheritance and wasted it, living his own life. But he'd come to his senses and returned home chastened. She'd lived her own life too. But how the father had welcomed back his son! And the one about the rich young ruler who told Jesus he had kept all the commandments, but to whom Jesus said, "Sell everything you have." That had really said something to her: she'd been a good person, too, but this commitment had to be total! Then there was the one about the children of Israel who had walked through the Red Sea because God was with them. She had her own Red Sea, and she would walk through it, too, *if* God was with her.

They quoted the book of John: "There are many rooms in my Father's house and I am going to prepare a place for you. . . . You cannot see God with your old nature, only with a new one. You must be born again." Another passage had also spoken volumes: "Remove my sin and I will be clean. Wash me and I shall be whiter than snow." She had prayed that verse as she started to read the Bible.

Then, about eighteen months after the accident, when she was alone, and for no reason that she could think of, she would suddenly feel she was about to burst with happiness. All through that summer, from out of nowhere, sometimes in the morning, sometimes in the afternoon, the extraordinary joy and lightness would come, and it was only later that she realized why: it was the lightness of heart that came from being "whiter than snow." About the same time she and Otto began going to church.

Marianne has her own perspective on the accident. Happening as it did only a few days after her birthday, it was nothing less than a divine birthday gift in her opinion. How could God send such a catastrophe as a gift? In her quiet, careful way she explains: "If it hadn't happened, life would have continued as it always had. I knew nothing about God. He had to shake me, because He loved me. It's only since the accident that life has become meaningful, that I am happy, that I'm no longer frightened of dying, and that God has become a Person I can love. Now I couldn't live without Him."

2
RE-PLAY

Victoria de Aguilar sits on the bed stunned, staring at the radio. She's never heard words like these before—words that seem to see right inside her.

Words that re-create vivid scenes of long ago—as if the moments had been captured by a camera and were being projected now onto some interior screen.

Incredulous, she slithers slowly off the bed onto her knees. It's the beginning of a silent movie show, but to an audience of only one. Slowly, as one clear image replaces another, remorse begins to well up like a tide inside her, until suddenly with all her might she wants to scream out, "I'm sorry, forgive me!"

The images have no speech, but their silent language is more eloquent than words, each adding its own damning indictment until pardon seems impossible. She flings herself over the bed in a paroxysm of despair, begging for mercy, but the show doesn't stop. For half an hour, the images move with relentless and silent force onto the internal screen in her mind, each tapping its own deep spring of desperate entreaty.

She is exhausted when the strange spectacle ends; and she drags herself slowly off the bed, her eyes red and swollen, her throat hoarse from crying and shouting. She walks unsteadily to the door, parting the flimsy, white lace curtain separating her bedroom from the corridor, and stands there, no longer sobbing, but the tears still wet on her cheeks.

Suddenly an unaccountable and extraordinary feeling of exhilaration takes her. She feels as light as air, as light as a spring breeze. She begins to run like a child, up and down the green-painted concrete corridor, her feet barely touching the ground, running until she is completely out of breath, then sinking down on a couch, gasping and laughing. As she regains her breath it seems she can breathe more deeply, and her shoulders feel inches higher—as if a tremendous weight has been lifted off them.

Victoria de Aguilar laughs in the retelling. It all happened seven years ago, but it's still as fresh as yesterday.

For thirty years Victoria was a prostitute. But it's hard to imagine. This calm, contented, good-looking, olive-skinned woman of fifty-three with smooth, Spanish features, sitting close to her husband, looks for all the world like a woman who's been married to the same man all her life—and one who's always treated her well.

Victoria started life in Caracas, Venezuela, gasping for air. She had asthma almost from the day she was born, the third in a poor and illiterate family of seven. Her mother went to spiritists for potions and spells to cure her, but nothing worked. Her asthma made schooling almost impossible—so she was kept home to keep house while her mother worked for a few extra bolivars. If she did a careless job, her father beat her. He used to beat them all, including her mother, who suspected his unfaithfulness because he spent so many of his evenings dancing. When she went to the spiritist for cures for Victoria, she also bought spells to bring her husband home nights.

Victoria was thirteen when she tore herself away from her father as he was about to thrash her for a poor ironing job on his shirt. "Don't worry," she flashed at him, "you'll never have to thrash me again! I'm leaving!" It was just a threat, but as she ran out the front gate, she saw the boy across the road leaning against a gate post watching her. She'd always liked the look of him; he was twenty-two and handsome. She slowed down, gave him a coy look, and stopped to talk.

"Like a spin in my Cadillac?" He jerked his head toward his big, shiny car. "Just around the block."

"All right," she said, "but we can't be gone for long. I've got to be back home early."

He took her out, then on the way back stopped at a soda fountain and bought her a little glass of liquid. "Drink it," he encouraged. She tried it, expecting a soda. It was very sweet. "Drink it all," he said.

So she did, and by the time she drained the glass her head was spinning. "I'll take you back to the house," she heard him say, and she tried to stand up but couldn't. The last thing she remembered was being helped to the car. Everything was a blank until she awoke the next morning. She screamed, aghast, "Look what you've done to me! How can I ever go home again?"

"Don't worry," he said. "I'll take you somewhere else." And he took her to the home of a young couple.

Her mother and the police found her several days later. They knew about the racket run by the boy, his brother, and his father and figured out what had happened: drugging, then raping. It was illegal, but the racket still went on because the trio had money, and money bought immunity. The civil chief said it was all Victoria's fault and she would have to marry the boy, who claimed she wasn't a virgin anyway (though a medical examination showed she was). They were married in a civil ceremony, and Victoria went back to her parents' to wait for him, but he never arrived. Nor did he return to the neighborhood. Three days later her parents turned Victoria out—a thirteen-year-old who didn't know how to catch a bus or hail a taxi and who had nowhere to live.

She went back to the young couple's, but they didn't want her. So her party-loving older sister took her in. Later, at the age of fifteen, she found herself pregnant by a seventeen-year-old who said he loved her but changed his mind when he found out she was pregnant. Her sister pushed her out; there was no room in their already crammed quarters for a baby. So Victoria went from friend to relative until her son was born, then tried to find work. But no one wanted to employ an unskilled, asthmatic woman with a baby. Her father, now separated from her mother, took her in for three months but tossed her out because the baby cried too much and she refused to let anyone adopt him.

"Could you give me twelve bolivars for a can of milk for my baby?" she asked a woman on the street one day, never guessing what her innocent question would lead to.

The woman looked her up and down. "You're asking me for a can of milk when you've got a body like yours?" she said reproachfully to Victoria.

And so Victoria was introduced to organized prostitution, though not without a struggle. "I didn't want to be a prostitute. I fought like a cat," she says. "They literally had to hold me down." But their logic won in the end; she was young and unskilled, and she had a baby. What else could she do? The oldest profession in the world would pay her well, and in addition the girls would look after her baby while she earned.

So Madam taught her how to perform her own abortions with a probe, and Victoria learned the profession. But the work was sordid, and she drank heavily with clients to numb her senses. By the age of twenty-five she had lost count of the number of times she had performed her own abortions. But she decided to let one of the pregnancies go to term, and her second child—a daughter—was born.

The girls treated her well; when a doctor had to operate to remove gall stones and an appendix, the other prostitutes nursed her back to work. Her mother finally tracked her down and encouraged her to remain a prostitute. The money was good, she said, but could be better if she went to the spiritists for spells and potions to make her more beautiful. "Then you'll make enough money to put the children in the best schools in Caracas and to support me as well," she said. So Victoria often visited occult practitioners, and sometimes their incantations and potions seemed to work.

But often she felt sad, depressed, and lonely, and sometimes she went to church and confessed to the priests. Usually they gave her prayers to say and penances to do, and advised her to give up prostitution and do as much good as she could. One old priest conceded she had to earn her bread and butter somehow, but he prescribed charitable works to balance the ledger. So Victoria burned candles and kept images of the saints and spiritists for good luck. Christian or occult, what was the difference? They would all help bring health, good fortune, and men who paid well.

And she did get good clients, and they did pay her well—enough for her to buy a car and receive the best medical treatment. But in spite of it her nerves were driving her crazy, and she was smoking two or three packs of cigarettes a day.

She was forty when she conceived again—an ectopic pregnancy this time, and when the fallopian tubes burst, it was touch and go. She had three cardiac arrests in the operating room. But she recovered and once out of the hospital decided to move west along the coast to a spot where the air was better. She chose Puerto Cabello and bought a house in the center of town. One of her clients, Baudilio Aguilar, moved in with her. He trucked produce around the region during the week, and on weekends they drank together.

But a change of air did nothing for Victoria's depression, and she often felt "tormented, sad, and empty." A psychiatrist gave her pills and an injection for the incessant pain in her chest. But it didn't make any difference, except to make her feel drugged and lethargic. One of her men told her to try marijuana, and she did but didn't like it.

Then the stitches from the operation began to pull out, and she began feeling sick. Awake and nauseated early one morning, she reached for the radio, as she often did when she didn't feel well; the music helped revive her spirits. It was 5:00 A.M., January 1978, and she picked up a strong medium wave signal: *El Tiempo Aceptable* they said the program was. She listened, fascinated, and wondered how it was she could feel guilty and yet so relieved at the same time.

She took note of the next broadcast and listened regularly for the following few weeks, noticing that whenever she listened she felt peaceful. She took fewer pills and didn't go to the psychiatrist so often. But the feelings of guilt intensified, and often Baudilio would come home and find her crying.

"What they were saying was reaching right inside me, and I was seeing my life, and it was awful," Victoria says. She is sitting on a bench at the head of the long corridor in her home, with Baudilio lounging in a seat alongside, listening. "I knew that I had been very bad and that my past was terrible—but I didn't understand what I had to do."

She decided to enroll in a Bible study course offered by *El Tiempo Aceptable*, and as she worked through the course her sense of shame and guilt intensified. Three months after she first tuned in, she heard the program that threw the images of her life so unexpectedly and dramatically on screen. "When I got up off the bed, I was no longer the same person," she says. "I knew that God had taken my horrible, disastrous life and forgiven me. The joy and relief I felt was absolutely indescribable."

After she had run like a child up and down the corridor and sunk exhausted onto the settee, she went to the record player to play some of the mood music she usually put on when she was drinking—music to have a good time to. She wanted to celebrate. But she turned it off again almost immediately; it sounded discordant, jangling, and empty.

That wasn't the only thing that felt wrong that week. At the supermarket, as she reached for the usual ample supply of liquor and spirits, it seemed as if someone kept pulling her back from the shelves. Finally she gave up and didn't buy any.

It wasn't long before Victoria called Madam and told her, "I'm quitting; please don't send any more men." But Madam continued sending them, and Victoria continued to show them the door—the same door onto which she soon hammered a small notice: "Home produce sold here." She began to use her domestic skills to bake, cook, sew, buy, and resell to make a living by other means.

She didn't tell Baudilio what had happened. She didn't really know what to say. But it soon became obvious to him that the woman he was coming home to was a different person. "She was a whole lot happier," Baudilio says. He's a swarthy, good-looking Venezuelan, shorter than Victoria and eight years younger. "She started treating me better." It wouldn't have been hard to notice the difference: Victoria's temper was so fierce, she regularly broke chairs over his back and used to beat him every color of the rainbow with a stick—especially when he came home drunk. At times he disappeared for days to escape her fury. But Victoria gets upset at this talk. "Now we are happy," she says. "We live in peace with love."

So when Baudilio came home drunk and pitched onto the bed, Victoria no longer picked up her stick. Instead, she knelt by the bed and prayed for him, diving under the bed when he stirred and coming out to pray some more when he was still again.

By the time Baudilio started to eavesdrop on the programs, Victoria had already thrown out all her cigarettes. As he continued listening with her at odd times over the following five years, the same sense of sadness and shame came over him that Victoria had felt, and one day, when local evangelicals were holding meetings in the town, he decided to go and do what they kept suggesting on the programs. In a halting but heartfelt few words he asked God to forgive him and change him, and six days later he and Victoria were married. At the same time, local pastors prayed for Victoria's chronic asthma; it has never recurred since.

But Madam still had problems with Victoria's new status as a lady and kept sending men to her door. And Victoria kept surprising them. One man thought her refusals were just a coy pitch for more money. "If it's money you want," he said, "help yourself," and threw down a bag containing $7,000 (American money) in Venezuelan bank notes. Victoria refused, and the man left shaking his head. Client No. 2 left in high consternation when Victoria told him she was no longer in business but had become "una evanjelica." He stumbled backwards out the door, turned, and fled.

But the prize has to go to the man who, although he wasn't a regular at Victoria's door, wasn't a newcomer, either. "Hello. Victoria Damico, please," he said as she answered the door. He used her maiden name.

"Yes," she said. "I'm Victoria."

"Aaah . . . no, sorry," he said, looking at her slightly more closely. "Victoria Damico."

"But I am Victoria Damico," she repeated.

The conversation stuck there. The man left in confusion after a few moments, deciding to try another address. The house was right, but for sure, the woman was quite different!

3
JONAH

Wolfgang Baake's bulky six-foot frame resonates with bonhomie, enthusiasm, and good humor. He's out from behind his desk, booming greetings before you're even half way through the door, his hand extended and a wide, friendly grin on his face. He enjoys people.

He drops straight into a casual chair, throws his right ankle onto his left knee, and gestures to you with extended arm to sit down. You haven't been there long when giant cream cakes arrive, along with cups of coffee.

His desk is littered with paper. A large flag of the German Federal Republic spreads its black, red, and gold stripes across the rear office wall, and the mounted photographs of German church and state dignitaries reflect back at you. Wolfgang relates with all these people; it's his job. As director of Konferenz Evangelikaler Publizisten, he has to communicate the concerns of German evangelical churches to the media and politicians—and he thrives on it.

He would never have been offered the job—nor had the credentials to take it—if he hadn't turned on his radio at midnight one night ten years ago near the Arctic circle because he was lonely. But he was moving in top gear away from his conscience, because Wolfgang had the very strong and unhappy conviction that God wanted him to take a theological degree, and theological degrees were anathema to Wolfgang Baake. In complete frustration he'd thrown his yellow pup tent into his Volkswagen and driven like a fugitive two days north to the quiet

Finnish fir forests he loved—to camp alone, read, fish, cook over his camp-stove, and push the thought of theological studies as far from his mind as God was going to let him. He wasn't even going to let himself think about God, which was why he'd left his Bible behind, and he didn't plan to do any praying.

This would have disturbed his father had he known, because Wolfgang had had a solid German evangelical upbringing. In fact, Wolfgang adored his father and was very like him. He adored his father even more than he adored the other Bach, Johann Sebastian, the composer. His father was church organist, and Wolfgang, too, was musical, often venting his strong baritone up front at church and leading the church youth music group. For as long as he could remember, he had believed in Jesus Christ and, like his father, wanted to follow Him.

Like his father he was bright, but unlike him, he was lazy. Cars had a lot more appeal than studies for Wolfgang, and at sixteen he left school for a job with Volkswagen. He spent ten years in the foreign dispatch division of the parts department. The shop floor was his mission field, and when the subject came up, he talked openly and naturally about his faith. He usually spent his weekends preparing for the annual saloon car rallies, and four times he carried off first or second prizes in fields of up to one hundred entrants. Christ, Bach, and cars—the perfect trinity.

But at the age of twenty-five, he had a feeling that a change was ahead, and he went to a national Christian youth conference. The camp took its text from Psalm 86: "Teach me your way, O Lord, and I will walk in your truth." Wolfgang made the verse his prayer, and as he dipped into a book of daily Scripture readings at the camp one morning, a passage jumped out at him to add force to the first: "The Lord give grace to your journey —don't tarry." Then another verse: "Jesus saw Matthew sitting in his office, and said to him, 'Come, follow me.'" Then, as naturally as if someone had spoken in his ear, he knew exactly what he had to do: study for a theological degree. But the message had hardly hit home when all his instincts rose in armed revolt.

Wolfgang was no academic. He didn't want high-brow theology, thank you very much. He wanted a work-a-day faith that would rub off on his mates. The thought of poring over obscure textual criticisms in some dusty cloister gave him the cold horrors. He didn't want people organizing his day, and he didn't like studying. "If seminary is what You want me to do," he told God firmly, "You're going to have to push me in."

Back home he told his parents and a few friends, and to his consternation they thought it was a good idea, so he decided not to tell anyone else. But in the next four months, people who couldn't possibly have known what was in his mind kept saying to him, "Why don't you go to theological college?" And it was obvious which college it would have to be: Marbuch, only a hundred miles or so from home.

He felt more and more claustrophobic as the time for seminary applications drew near. "All right, if You insist!" he muttered, and sent for Marbuch's application forms. When they arrived he made sure he did a poor job on them. He'd heard the Academy had tough standards, and he didn't want to miss any opportunity to rule himself out. "I made deliberate typing mistakes and didn't correct them," Wolfgang grins. "I didn't give them the information I knew they wanted, or only gave a hint. I didn't tell them that I'd been raised in a Christian home. The whole thing was full of gaps and errors, and my writing was almost illegible."

But the ruse failed, and in six weeks he was asked to present himself for personal interviews. As he rose that morning, he made sure his appearance would help ruin his chances. Pushing aside suits and ties, he reached for his old denims, old shoes, casual open-necked shirt, and leather jacket. He smoked more than usual to make sure he smelt like an ash tray.

"I really did want to obey God," Wolfgang says, "but I wanted to be absolutely sure He was the one who got me in there, and no one else."

At Marbuch he talked with the dean and professors—the picture of studied indifference. They were long, thorough interviews, and a month later he heard to his disgust that he had been accepted for the fall term. He couldn't believe it. All he had to do was say yes, but he did nothing. Volkswagen wanted six months' notice of resignation, and there wasn't time to give it. Opening day was three months away.

June came and went, then July. August began, and still he
did nothing. September was only weeks away. "I just fervently
hoped it would all go away," Wolfgang says. "I hoped God would
say, 'It's OK, Wolfgang, I don't really want you to go.' And I
wanted to give Him all the time in the world to say it."

But God never did. Pressure continued from his friends and
relatives and from places he least expected it—"Until I just
couldn't stand it. Everyone was on to me: 'You have to go, you
have to go.' I just had to get away from it all. I wasn't washing up
with God. I was just hoping against hope that I hadn't heard
Him right."

And that was when he loaded up his Volkswagen Rabbit
and drove north into Finland's midnight sun for three weeks. "I
ran away from it all, like Jonah. I decided not to pray or read the
Bible. But I still wanted God to make it clear to me, so clear that
I had no doubt."

So he fished and cooked, camped and read, and meandered
around the forest roads for two weeks. Then one night he felt
homesick for no particular reason. He roamed about for a while,
then decided to listen to "Evangeliums Rundfunk" on his car radio at 9:30 P.M. and, afterwards, to the German news broadcast.

He had heard "Evangeliums Rundfunk" before—but didn't
listen often. That night the subject was guidance, and the speaker's words hit him like falling pinecones. Ten years later, without
a moment's hesitation, he can still come up with the words of the
Manfred Siebald song that said it all.

> There is a place where God wants you.
> There is something that only you can do.
> No one else can do it as well as you.
> If you ask God where He wants you
> Then He will show you
> The work he wants you to do.

"That was it," says Wolfgang. "And I knew it without a
shadow of doubt: Marbuch it was!" Wolfgang's mind was made
up the same instant. At first light the following day he packed
the car, cutting short his vacation by a week, and began the two-

day drive back to West Germany. To his astonishment his boss
at Volkswagen waived the six-month requirement of notice and
only asked for two weeks. For some reason the idea of Wolfgang's
studying theology appealed to him immensely, and he wanted to
help all he could.

At 7:30 A.M. September 11, 1976, Wolfgang stubbed out
his last cigarette (and a sixty-a-day habit), packed his car, and
headed for Marbuch Theological Academy.

But if he thought that obedience had assured a happy college debut, he was mistaken. His roommate made no attempt to
make him feel welcome, or to even greet him. "I thought at
theological seminaries everyone was meant to be loving and kind
and holy," Wolfgang says. "This was a shock."

A few more followed: no dating, bedtime at 10:00 P.M.,
lights-out at 10:30 P.M. And the crowning insult, he had to take
advice from juniors—eighteen-year-olds—just because they'd
been there longer than he had. In addition, every minute of his
day was ordered, and when he graduated they were still going to
dictate to him. "I couldn't go where I wanted, only where 'they'
were going to send me."

And no cigarettes was the final straw. Having given all his
spending money to a friend so he couldn't buy any more, he was
absolutely miserable. "I was so miserable that, after two weeks, I
got ready to leave. I even packed my bags." Then an old man of
eighty who worked at the seminary took him into his workroom
and gave him some advice. "I told him I wasn't getting along
with anybody, and he read me a Bible passage: 'Let us rid ourselves of everything that gets in the way and run with determina-
tion the race before us. Let us keep our eyes fixed on Jesus from
beginning to end.'"

"If you keep your eyes on Jesus, you won't see so many of
these irritating people and rules," the old fellow suggested.

Wolfgang took up the suggestion. "It was the answer I
needed at the time, so I unpacked my bags." And the following
months brought a different perspective: "I began to see the rules
were really aids to study and that I was there to study, so after six
months I buckled down and accepted it." He had corners

knocked off, and it reduced him to size. "I discovered I wasn't as important as I thought I was. I also learned not to put conditions on God and to be more creative in ways I let my light shine."

His assignment upon graduation was a two-year posting to West Berlin as church youth director to the city's mixed cultural bag of young people. Then, in 1982, he was asked to head up Konferenz Evangelikaler Publizisten. He accepted, and in the course of a three-month refresher in evangelization and psychology, again at Marbuch, he met his wife, Renate, a nurse at the seminary hospital.

They married, and a year later son number one came into the world, bellowing with the gusto that promised a true son of his father and a rich baritone later. Bach fanatic that he was, Wolfgang christened him Johannes Sebastian Baake, only just controlling the urge to spell his first name exactly after the eighteenth-century composer. It took all his father's influence to stop him.

But Wolfgang wasn't silly. Really, he knew only too well the risks of forcing an unwanted vocation on a son who might grow up to be the spitting image of his father.

4
EXECUTIVE

The local columnist made Marcey Brandt sound like the sort of woman everyone wanted to know: an "uproariously funny lady, a delight—a workaholic who made it all look like fun. She carried out the business of late millionaire Roy Carver with such style . . . that she made it look like a piece of cake. I rarely saw her when she wasn't involved in some sort of international deal, with endless phone calls to places with strange-sounding names. Marcey seemed like a lady with such energy and enthusiasm for life that she could live forever."

Marcey didn't. She died suddenly of a brain hemorrhage at age fifty-two, in August 1986, and the words were penned by a columnist writing her obituary. If Marcey had been looking over her shoulder, she would probably have snorted, because *she* always told the story differently.

While Marcey Brandt was jet-setting around the world, doing business with oil sheikhs in the Persian Gulf, and managing her boss's properties in Europe and the Americas, his fleets of airplanes and his yachts, she showed one face to the world. The other one, no one saw. She hid it from everyone, including herself—mainly by keeping herself furiously occupied. "The minute I could see any excuse for business in another city or part of the world, I was on a jet and off," Marcey said about nine months before she died. "I was running because I knew that if I stopped I would have a confrontation that I didn't want. So I had to keep moving."

Marcey came to terms with herself on the French Riviera while she was trying to sell her boss's sprawling villa in Cannes. She had just disposed of his oil tanker to a Greek client and called Carver. "What do you want me to do now?"

And he had said, "Why not sell the villa in Cannes?"

"That may take a little time," she'd replied. It took longer than even she had bargained for: fourteen months. During that time she was almost a recluse, in a setting most people only dream about: a luxurious property on the blue Mediterranean, with personal chauffeur, gardener, maid, and secretary. But she spent the time coming to terms with the person behind the bright face, who was depressed, lonely, confused, and often in tears.

Marcey's malaise had started about nine months after her divorce—after the sense of freedom and enormous relief had gone. She was admitted to the hospital for tests. Six months later she was in again. "The doctors found nothing wrong except fatigue," Marcey says. "But that was all I wanted to know. It wasn't spiritual or emotional; it was physical. A psychiatrist came in and rubbed my hand and said, 'You'll be OK. It's just that your divorce is hitting you.'" She had violent headaches, and her legs felt like rubber. But Marcey put all the medicine they gave her under the bed. "I wouldn't even take an aspirin. I told them to leave me alone and let me sleep it all off. I stayed there sixteen days and did a lot of sleeping. I came out very weak from being in bed so long, but I felt fantastically well."

She was at work the following day, just in time for a call from Carver. "When can you go to Athens to sell our oil tanker?"

"Tomorrow," said Marcey immediately, and the next day she was en route to Greece.

She took a taxi to her hotel, shut the door to her room, and immediately started crying. "I was worn out, and I was lonely. I said to myself, 'What in the world am I doing in Athens? I've never been here in my life, I don't know anyone, and where do I start to sell an oil tanker?'"

For no particular reason she'd packed a Bible. Now she rummaged around for it, opened it at random, and tried to read. But she couldn't stop crying, and nothing she read sank in. But in the telephone directory, she found the word "Baptist" and arranged to go the following morning to a little Southern Baptist church just outside Athens. But the taxi driver got lost, and she never made it. She telephoned the pastor, however, and two days later he showed her around Corinth and Athens, using the Bible as part commentary. Marcey was interested because she didn't know much about the Bible.

Marcey was one of six children from a poor family. Her mother was an active Baptist, but her father wasn't interested, though if the kids didn't go to Sunday school they weren't allowed out to play. As they grew older, there was a ban on smoking and drinking. She was baptized at twelve, became an active member of the youth group, then its president. But her best friends weren't interested in church, and at the age of nineteen she married a man two years older who wasn't interested either. Ten days later he left to fight in Korea for eighteen months, and when he returned they were strangers and fought a lot. It didn't help when the doctors told her she would never be able to have children. Her close relationship with her own family, and the care and attention she lavished on them when her mother died, added jealously to injury.

"I was torn," Marcey says. "I was never a person to fight; I would withdraw rather than argue. So I didn't learn to communicate with him. We had a lot of barriers, and I carried a lot inside me." But she found relief by throwing herself into work: "The more they gave me the more I would offer to do. I could never be busy enough."

Then the chance came to adopt a baby girl—Lori. "I guess we thought this was what would make us happy and strengthen our marriage," says Marcey. "But I found out when I was at home with her that I wasn't happy. I wanted to work." But it came time to take Lori to Sunday school, so Marcey started going to church again. Her husband came too, was baptized, and made a profession of faith. "I thought, Now we'll have a stable home," Marcey says, "but our home life didn't change one bit. I tried to start prayer and Bible study, but he just got angry, and after a week he put a stop to it all. So I withdrew again and stayed home till Lori started school."

Meanwhile she had become president of the Baptist Women's Missionary Group, church youth director—organizing summer camp for forty teen-agers—and Sunday school teacher.

When Lori started school Marcey returned to work, on a part-time basis, against her husband's wishes. But the business was growing; she was offered the position of company secretary. She resigned after six months—unable to bear the strain of an unhappy marriage—but Carver wouldn't hear of it. He asked her to manage his private business interests, and Marcey accepted. But then Carver became a millionaire overnight when he listed his private international company on the New York Stock Exchange—and everything changed.

"Roy Carver suddenly had so much money," Marcey says. "He bought airplanes, yachts, a villa on the French Riviera, 24,000 acres in Central America, a huge condominium in Miami. And as his estate grew I was taking responsibility for everything. I did the buying, selling, decorating, managing, staffing. I started out a secretary in a small office; I was now manager of a complex international corporation."

But the marriage was in ruins. In 1976 Marcey flew to Qatar with two other directors of the corporation to tie up an oil concession with the Qatar government. She went in one of Carver's private executive jets—a luxuriously refitted BAC 111, and the invitation was extended to her husband, too, but he angrily declined. Breaking the return journey at Carver's villa at Cannes, Marcey received a blistering phone call from him. "If you're not home in twenty-four hours, that's it," he said.

"We'd had a lot of problems to that point," Marcey says, "but we'd never discussed divorce, because we were both so busy. I hung up and said, 'Well, that's it.' It's like the cord had been severed. I got back to the States about three days later, and there was nothing there. We tried to communicate, but I had nothing to say. I had already set my compass, and I wasn't going to deviate. Within a week we separated, and I continued traveling for Carver."

But she was increasingly unhappy. "Deep down inside I knew I was wrong, but I could justify all my actions. It wasn't my fault, and it wasn't my responsibility. It was the way I had been treated. I was all right, and my life was OK. I didn't want anyone telling me I was wrong. I didn't want anyone to talk to me. I didn't want to go to church, but I went sometimes. When I sat in the pew I felt coldness all around me. Nobody wanted to associate with me, and I thought, *How pious of them.* Two church officers visited during the separation, but no one else from the church came. I thought, *They don't care. No one's interested in me.* But the truth was, I didn't want any answers at that point. I wasn't interested in talking to them."

Alone in the vast villa at Cannes, fresh from her tour of Greek antiquities, Marcey asked her secretary to send over some reading material from the States. "I'd belonged to this Christian book club, and I had all their books and the magazines but I hadn't read them. Really, I'd surrounded myself with Christian literature, but it didn't mean anything; it was a kind of security blanket, the thing to do—the right thing to do."

From April to December Marcey closeted herself in the villa, reading her books and magazines and listening to tapes. "I didn't go out and make friends with anyone, because I didn't want to go wining and dining. I couldn't speak any French, and I didn't know where to find any Americans." But she decided to go to church—the only English-language church she could find. It was Anglican and a shock to the system. "I was a Baptist. I was used to a twenty-five minute message. But the vicar only gave about a three minute message. It was good, but all this kneeling and getting up and down was far far away from what I was used to. I became very critical. To me there wasn't going to be anybody in heaven but a Baptist, and if they didn't go to the First Baptist Church of Muscatine, Iowa, they'd never make it either. That's what I thought, and yet, in all my years I was never sure I was going to get there myself."

The villa still refused to sell, and Marcey was a prisoner in a palace, confused, lonely, and desperately wanting company and advice. "One Sunday night—it was midnight—I was very lonely. I was lying in bed with my tiny little radio on my chest, about to burst into tears. I said, 'God, if only there were some way of communicating with You so that I could get some help or guidance.' Then I flipped the switch on the radio, and instantly there was this program, "Radio Bible Class," from Trans World Radio, Monte Carlo. I didn't know what it was—I wasn't even sure where Monte Carlo was—but it was in English. I listened to the whole program and cried all the way through. It was about not being critical of other churches and to worship in them without criticism. It made me realize that I could go to the Anglican church without feeling like a traitor and that God could even speak to me through Anglican hymns, Anglican prayers, and an Anglican sermon. That was a breakthrough—until then God could only speak to me through the sermon of a Baptist preacher.

"So I kept going to the Anglican church, and one morning I saw a set of heads in the front of me that didn't look English or French." Marcey made their acquaintance—a United States family—and spent a weekend with them some months after a trip to the Mediterranean island of Majorca to sell one of Carver's twin yachts—a 135-footer. "I was in the pits," Marcey says, "really depressed, so this weekend these people went through my life together. And finally Donna said, 'Marcey, you've never been saved.' That cut to the quick, because I was headed for heaven. I said, 'I just can't believe that, Donna.' My little Baptist faith wouldn't buy it."

Marcey went home that evening, put on one of the tapes and started reading the Bible. "I was in Galatians—and it was talking about the sins of the flesh and the fruit of the Spirit. When I read about the sins of the flesh, you don't know how sick I felt inside. It was a picture of me: 'people become enemies and they fight; they become jealous, angry and ambitious. . . .' But I said to myself, 'No, I'm OK. I'm a do-gooder,' until I came to the verse which said, 'those who do these things will not possess the Kingdom of God.' And I thought at that moment, *I'm not going to heaven!* And I tell you, I was scared. Then I read about the fruit of the Spirit—love and kindness, gentleness, patience, goodness—and tears welled up. I said, 'But God, that's the way I want to be.' It was what I had always thought I was, but I knew at that instant that I wasn't. I saw myself as God saw me. So I got down on my knees, and in my mind I took my whole life—all of me, all my assets and all of my liabilities, all of my sins, all my selfishness and this big letter 'I'—and laid it out before God. I asked Him to forgive me and to clean me up. I said, 'Everything I have is Yours, and from now on my life is Your life. You can do whatever You want. If You want to take me home tonight, I'm ready.'"

She got off her knees, suddenly exhilarated. "I was so excited: I *knew* I was saved. I called Donna and some friends in America who I knew had been praying for me. I'd shelved them because I didn't want them interfering in my life-style. From that night on I was no longer afraid of dying, and my life has never been the same."

Marcey sold the villa and cabled her boss. Carver told her to stay on for another three months and manage his other yacht. "Can I base it in Monte Carlo?" Marcey asked. "Sure, anywhere you like," Carver said. So Marcey lived at anchor in Monaco harbor and became firm friends with the staff members of Trans World Radio, whose program she had picked up that Sunday night. One of the organization's stations operated out of Monaco. "They heard my story, and they started teaching me and befriending me, and it was the delight of my life to be with them."

After three months Marcey decided to quit her job with Carver. She returned to the States, called Carver in Florida, and told him she had to see him. He said, "Fine." So Marcey flew down. "It was the night before he was going to leave on a three-week business trip to Europe," Marcey says. "I sat him down and said, 'I'm going to quit. I'm going to go into full-time Christian work.' He couldn't understand why that was more important than all the money and all the projects I could be involved in, so I tried to explain it. He listened; he was very interested. I said, 'It can happen for you too.' He leaned forward and said, 'No, not tonight. We'll talk about it one of these days.' I said, 'Are you going to wait until you're on your deathbed?' He said, 'No, I'll talk to you before then,' and the next day he left for Europe. Two weeks later I had a telephone call from his doctor in Iowa who said that my boss had just suffered a fatal heart attack."

Within hours Marcey was executor of an estate worth between $200 and $300 million. It took more than a year to settle, and as it wound up, the pangs of loneliness began to return again. "I got down on my knees alongside my bed and said, 'Lord I'm so lonely. I've always been a doer and a putter-together, and now the estate is wrapping up, and I don't have anything to challenge me. My husband has remarried, and I don't like being alone. I really want someone to love and someone to care for me. But if you don't want me to marry again, then help me live alone as a loving, compassionate person. I don't want to feel sorry for myself.' Then I got up from my knees, and I had a great peace about it," Marcey says. "I never thought about it again."

But someone else did. Several months later a lawyer friend rang her long distance. "There's this man who's just lost his wife," he said. "He's lonely. I think it'd be good for you to talk to him."

"I said, 'Charlie, you know I'm really not interested in meeting anybody. Is he in your office?' He said, 'No, just hold on a minute.' So Charlie Morgan called Dr. Henry Brandt in Florida and said, 'Henry, I've got this woman I'd like you to meet. She's lonely. I think it'd be good for you to talk to her.' And Dr. Brandt said, 'Charlie, I'm really not interested.'"

So began a courtship between Dr. Henry Brandt, Christian consulting psychologist, seminar speaker and author, and Marcella McKillip, a millionaire's personal assistant. Eleven months later they were married.

Marcella's life-style hardly changed. Her husband's speaking agenda was as whirlwind as her own itinerary had been. They were together three years. Then Marcella died, very suddenly, just after she had finished telling her story to some friends. Her last words were that she was no longer frightened of dying. Then she said she felt very strange. Her friends laid her on the floor, and she lost consciousness. She never regained it.

Dr. Brandt wrote to his friends some months after her death: "Almost as quick as the twinkling of an eye, God took her. We had been inseparable for three years. She was a cheery companion. I am only beginning to appreciate all she did for me and with me. God allowed me to have these years with Marcey. I am so thankful for that. Now there is a huge hole. God has equally wonderful plans for the rest of my days. I anticipate the future eagerly and happily as He gives me vision and strength. The future is in God's steady, loving hands."

You can almost imagine Marcey reading over his shoulder, giving it a squeeze, and saying, "That's right, Doctor."

5
OLD ROCKS

"Sometimes a rock has to be struck with a hammer many times before it cracks and splits right open." (A native American)
He could have added, "Sometimes the rock might be so old and hard that you almost give up."

Arne and Sven had very little in common except their nationality, their age, and their sex—and a certain bottleneck in their thinking. They were both Swedish, both elderly, and both male. And they both had real difficulty making much sense of what they heard on HCJB. Not that they didn't *want* to believe; it's just that their minds threw up so many objections, they couldn't.

Arne was retired, a former personal photographer to the Swedish royal family. The walls of his home in Stockholm were decked with black and white photos of his royal subjects. Sven had been an artist in his own way too: an organ builder. But his lungs had been wrecked by a chemical he had inhaled most of his working life. Both men were prolific correspondents and long-term listeners to HCJB's short-wave Scandinavian service from Quito.

Arne's first letter to HCJB arrived suddenly, and its tone was to characterize his letters for years. "I write as an agnostic. I cannot believe what you say about God and His son, Jesus Christ." It was the beginning of a long association with Arne, by mail and radio; often programmers replied to his questions on air.

Trying to convince him that God was good, HCJB once sent him their entire correspondence file with another Swedish listener on the same subject. Another load of letters to a young listener on Arne's favorite theme, "How do you know Christianity is right?" also winged their way to Arne's private address. Arne returned most of it, underlining the sections he took exception to and scratching in the margins in his bold hand: "This isn't true!" "Nobody can be sure of this!" "History teaches us something different here!"

Arne's wife used to write, too. She was badly bothered by her conviction that God would judge her children and her grandchildren for her sins, that Jesus Christ could not remove them. Nothing the staff wrote would change her mind.

Sven the organ builder also wrote copiously, but little survives of his correspondence. "I know I need to understand my relationship with God," he wrote. "I just cannot make it apply to me, to my former life." His letters remained full of questions.

Then came time for personal visits back home for a Swedish programmer, Sonja, and she visited Arne and his wife in Stockholm, only to find Arne's wife dying of a cancer of the throat, capable only of unintelligible noises. But Arne understood her and acted as go-between. In a long three-way conversation that afternoon, Sonja and Arne's wife laid to rest her fears that God would not forgive her, and at the end Arne translated for his wife: "Sonja, that's wonderful news."

Wonderful for his wife, but not for Arne. After she died he moved into a rest-home for the elderly and continued to fill his letters with pages of objections. As he aged he remained alert and curious, but on a later visit Sonja was told to expect to find him slightly senile and confused. Old and very frail, yes; but confused, no. He was sitting at his desk as she entered, and he recognized her immediately.

He was the first to speak. "Well, Sonja, so you've come to see me. That's good." Then he turned and reached up to his desktop calendar and with his thin fingers traced the words as he read them with obvious pleasure. "I am the Light of the world. Whoever follows me will never walk in darkness but will have the Light of Life." He turned to Sonja and smiled. "I imagine you have come to speak to me about that Light?"

Naturally Sonja had, but the old rock had already split wide open. For the first time Sonja could recall, Arne was no longer arguing. He could now repeat his dying wife's words, "Sonja, that's wonderful news."

And Sven? When he heard Sonja was coming to Sweden, he wrote and begged her to visit. "I hope I will live till you come. Please talk with me personally," he pleaded. "I must find peace with God." Sonja had only two days free before the start of a month of demanding commitments. She debated seeing Sven then or leaving it till later. She decided to see Sven that weekend, and called his number. Someone else answered: "Please come, he's waiting for you. He's a very sick man." Sonja came and sat with Sven. Together they spent three hours working through the theology of salvation, until Sven's face suddenly lit up and his voice cracked with joy: "I see it, I see it."

Sonja completed her assignment, and a month later, back in Stockholm, she called Sven again. The same kind voice answered that she had heard the first time. "Ah, Sonja, I'm so glad you've called. Sven left us last night."

6
BELIEVER

Believer! Fifteen-year-old Tapio cringed whenever he heard the word. The last thing he wanted to be was a believer. All he wanted to be was normal. Normal and liked. But believers weren't liked, and they certainly weren't normal.

He could see them now: funny people who didn't know how to enjoy themselves and who didn't like it if *you* did. Always gloomy about something, narrow-minded, always praying and telling you what not to do. Old fashioned.

He winced as he imagined what people would think of him if he became an *Uskovainen*—a believer. *Believer* was a byword in Finland. It wouldn't just embarrass his parents and relatives; he'd lose all his friends. It upset him a lot that the radio used the same sort of language the believers did: being "born again" and "accepting Christ as your Savior." If being "born again" meant becoming a believer, then Tapio wasn't going to have an ounce of it. But, even so, he liked what they said on the radio—Billy Graham and the others—and he always thought a lot about what they said.

He had always been interested in God, ever since he was small, and whenever he listened he felt part of a big, warm, invisible brotherhood. It made him want to do something about it, but then they'd go and say something that made them sound just like the believers.

Tapio was, as he wanted to be, an ordinary Finnish boy, but he was also what he did not want to be, painfully shy and quiet, and always wondering what people thought of him. It was so important to him to be liked that when he was eleven he joined a gang of young neighborhood toughs and started drinking and smoking. But really he only played around on the edges—didn't get into anything too tough. He only joined in the first place because his best friend wanted him to, and who wants to lose his best friend?

But it didn't do him any good. His grades at school nosedived, he was hardly ever home, and his parents were worried sick about him. He could see for himself after a while that he hadn't made any new friends; apart from a couple of fellows in the gang, no one else liked him. It was obvious—they just ignored him. He had a bad conscience about his activities and what he was doing to his parents: good, hard-working Lutherans —like most of Finland's churchgoers. They didn't like the idea of becoming believers either.

So he'd made his decision: he left the gang and stayed around home more. It wasn't easy. He argued with his parents and fought with his brother, but it was a sight more comfortable than gang life. And if he hadn't been at home he would probably never have flicked the switch on the family radio one night and discovered a fascinating new world of shortwave. It became a hobby that engrossed him by the hour, and his self-confidence soared when he realized one day at school that he had become a specialist in something most others in his class knew nothing about. It rubbed off on his grades, and only months later he was the top student in his class. His parents did everything to encourage his new interest and bought him a new shortwave radio set, which was how he'd picked up the religious radio programs, listening first to improve his English, but then to hear the program —and struggling with the concepts and terminology the programs shared in common with those awful believers.

Then the local Lutheran Boy's Club leader asked him to help two hours a week, and Tapio accepted because he'd attended Boy's Club himself when he'd been a kid. He organized games and quizzes and told Bible stories, and enjoyed doing it. Six months later he was of age to be confirmed a full member of the Lutheran church, and he waited eagerly for the classes to begin.

But he was astonished at his reactions when the classes did start. He felt defensive, stubborn, and self-conscious. "I was sure no one accepted me, and I couldn't stop thinking, 'What are these people thinking of me?'" he says. "If my eyes met someone else's I would plunge into confusion and introspection."

Here he had his first encounter with people who should have been believers, but weren't. They weren't narrow minded and disapproving, and they didn't dress in old fashioned clothes. They were fun. And they didn't seem to care if people confused them with the believers. Fifteen-year-old Tapio liked them. "I knew I wasn't an atheist," he says, "but they were different from me. When I looked at them I knew I was lacking something. The more I observed them, the more I wanted to be like them—and the more I realized that I had only wanted to follow Jesus Christ from a distance."

As he kept attending the confirmation classes, he began to pray, using the language his new friends, the radio programs, and the believers had in common. "God, if You really exist, and if You love me and have something You want to do with me, please come into my heart and be my Savior. Even if I lose my friends, please come into my heart." He prayed the same prayer every night for one week but nothing outstanding happened—except he became aware over several days that God *had* forgiven him and that there was something new about the way he was living.

He found he wanted to read the Bible, and he knew he was behaving less self-conscious. A friend told him he was different. He began to feel these were the signs that showed he had become a "true Christian." At least that was what he called himself, though other people saw it differently. In their eyes he had now become a believer—though Tapio was interested to find that this didn't upset him half as much as he thought it would.

Back at school he didn't get the ribbing he expected from his classmates either. One way and another his new convictions slowly became obvious, but the other young people seemed to accept him well enough. Predictably they all called him a believer, but by that stage Tapio really didn't care at all.

7
PROFILES

Samira and Miriam live in the Middle East, less than 50 kilometers from each other, but are total strangers. Samira is young, beautiful, aristocratic, wealthy, and ambitious. Miriam is old, lined, and slow, but gentle and satisfied, a mother of five, and now a great-grandmother.

Samira is married to a young doctor with a growing practice in the capital city. She has a boy and a girl—a fashionably-sized urban family. Samira and her husband are both Muslim, his family stricter than hers. Samira is slender, light-skinned, blond, and green-eyed—the envy of many of her swarthier countrywomen. She can dress to kill and knows it; her husband is often jealous. But the marriage is tempestuous for other reasons: Samira is demanding and contentious. She won't change an opinion for anybody, even if she is wrong, and the thought of rendering the traditional submissive obedience expected of a dutiful Muslim wife fills her with smoldering contempt. The marital rows are known to be explosive, and Samira has a dirty mouth. She tells a friend that her life is miserable—and it makes no sense, because she has everything.

During Easter Samira is bored and, for a bit of diversion, flicks the controls on the television set. It might be because she has a Christian friend that she leaves the set on the special Easter broadcast: Middle East Television's staple fare for its Christian minority during a major Christian festival.

She sees a re-enactment of the crucifixion, and it's strange that she is not only fascinated but moved to tears. She telephones her Christian friend; they've been close for five years, ever since their husbands started their joint medical practice. The couple have often come to help them sort out their rows. "What's going on?" Samira asks her friend. "I'm crying because I saw the cross. I'm upset. Why am I upset? Why should it affect me like this? It's just a cross."

The incident develops into a torrent of questions over the following weeks—mainly in long sessions over the telephone; Samira wouldn't dare go to church. But her friend hasn't got all day to talk. "Why don't you listen to Monte Carlo's Arabic broadcasts?" her friend tells her, and gives her times and frequencies. So Samira starts a regular listening habit, morning and evening. She also borrows Christian books, gets hold of a Bible, squirrels in cassettes of Christian speakers—everything in secret so her husband won't know. And when difficulties come up she's on the phone to her friend: "Pray for me and read to me from the Psalms."

Over the space of a year her husband notices a change in his wife: she's less willful and angry, more reasonable, dresses more modestly. Her language has cleaned up, and she's stopped smoking. "What's going on?" he asks the Christian couple. "I like it. She's easier to live with." He encourages the contact between the two women. "It's doing you good," he mentions to Samira.

Samira tells her husband nothing. If she does, his parents will probably put pressure on him to divorce her. But now he wants to know exactly what's behind the change.

Fifty kilometers away Miriam has lived with her husband, Saliba, for almost sixty years. Saliba was a landowner and, until he was seventy-five, owner of a small grocery store in his historic village. Three months ago he suffered a severe coronary that put him flat on his back, though now he is slowly recovering.

Old Miriam and Saliba's marriage has weathered all the shocks a family of five can throw at it, plus all the economic vi-

cissitudes and instability of decades of Middle East political
turmoil.

Saliba's name means *cross*, Miriam's means *Mary*—names
that mark them everywhere as members of the country's historic
Christian minority. Their commitment to the faith founded on
Palestinian soil 2,000 years ago runs very deep, like Abraham's,
and as a couple and family it has united them closely. Until Saliba had his coronary, they went every Sunday to the local evangelical church to worship and give their tithe. They had raised
their family of five to do the same; until now they were all educated and successful adults raising their kids to do it, too. Most of
them had studied for higher degrees overseas, and one son was
now a clinical pathologist, another a pharmacist.

Life had been busy and the days full for Saliba and Miriam
—running the business, raising the family, and, typical of that
culture, dispensing large dollops of hospitality to strangers. Their
home is still the favorite family meeting place. Though the kids
have long since left home, four generations gather there every
Sunday for dinner, to talk, laugh, and pick with their fingers at
the soft meats wrapped in vegetable leaves.

When Saliba had his coronary, Miriam hardly left his side.
For months she nursed him carefully back to health. But it meant
she couldn't get to the Sunday services, and she missed the messages, the singing, and the fellowship. That was when the broadcasts had come into their own, after she had come across them
unexpectedly eight years earlier when she was flipping across the
band just to see what was on. They were talking about Ruth, an-
cestor of King David, and she'd listened then and ever since.
While Saliba had been sick, the programs had been a Godsend.
They'd been able to listen quietly together, uninterrupted, and it
had been good, building into their quiet trust an even stronger
confidence that when death came, better things awaited.

When Saliba is better, they will be able to go back to
church again. Until then, they have each other, their family,
and the radio.

Miriam and Samira probably still live fifty kilometers apart in the Middle East and probably still know nothing about each other. But now one common thread unites them: a deeply ingrained radio listening habit.

8
GLUM CHUM

Ninth graders don't usually agree on a whole lot, but about
Mamiko Takagi they were of one mind: she was the third
gloomiest kid in the class. They put it to the vote, and there it
was: Mamiko the Gloomy. Not exactly the kind of label a fourteen-year-old Japanese teen-ager wants to hang on herself.

But it was true, and it was exactly how she felt—gloomy.
She was just a misfit: good at nothing except keeping to herself.
Clumsy, no good at sports; thin and gawky, she was tall for a Japanese fourteen-year-old: 5'10". Her height made her feel conspicuous—even though the other girls envied her.

Being at one of the city's academically elite schools didn't
help; it made even good work look poor. Others streaked past her
in the lessons, while she was always making mistakes and getting
sub-average grades. She failed the entrance examination to the
senior high school of her first choice, when most of the others
flew through.

She couldn't make conversation; the words came out all
wrong, or didn't come at all. When her name came up for a
council position, they made her librarian, and she always turned
crimson with embarrassment whenever she had to give her report
and fumbled everything she said. Often she had to repeat herself.
She was completely tongue-tied when she had to say anything in
public or even in front of small groups.

In the family it was the same. She'd been her father's favorite until he died, but as the youngest of four, she always felt the

others were treated more favorably than she was, and they always got better grades at school.

She could count the friends she had on the fingers of one hand. It had been like that ever since she was small; there'd never been anyone to play with. Now, in the part of the city of Sapporo where she lived on the northern island of Hokkaido, there were no students from her class living near, so she spent her time at home reading books and sketching.

But even at school she didn't join in the conversations of the few friends she did have; their talk seemed trivial—about how pretty they were, the latest pop stars, and hit songs. She liked classical music and jazz, and the works of the literary greats: the moral conflicts of André Gide or the dark humor of Japan's own Osamu Dazai. For her extracurricular activity she chose 'shogi,' Japanese chess—not because she liked chess but because she didn't know what else to choose.

Life was silent and lonely. "At junior high, I would quietly enter the classroom in the morning," she says. "At lunch-break I couldn't join in the chatter. I would quietly read a book all by myself, even though I got nothing out of it. And at the end of each day I would go quietly home. Sometimes someone beside me would ask if it was boring to be alone all the time, and I would feel so lonely and sad that I would almost burst into tears. But I would always say, 'No, I like doing this more.' I always regretted it afterwards. I should really have said that I was lonely. But that was how I was: unsociable, and shy, and a poor talker. And nothing ever went right."

She often thought no one would even notice if she quietly disappeared. Certainly no one would care even if they did notice. She looked forward to senior high. Perhaps at a new school something might be different—something might change. Something *had* to change. Life couldn't go on like this forever.

She was fourteen or fifteen when she discovered her brother's old shortwave radio in the storage cupboard, covered with dust, and in one of his shortwave radio magazines lying around the house she found she could get a QSL card—a special acknowledgment—if she listened to a sending station for a while and wrote them a reception report.

So she turned on the old radio, and among a lot of static, Chinese, and gibberish, she picked up a broadcast in Japanese from the Pacific island of Guam—someone called Pastor Hatori. She stayed tuned so she could give the program a rating the way the magazine said, then put pen to paper. "I heard Pastor Hatori on 'Voice of the Pacific.'" She wrote, giving times and her location: SINPO—5555. *

Staff sent back a QSL card, and she sent in some more reception reports. They sent her some literature and a Bible. It was inevitable, as she listened to give a rating, that she heard a lot of what was said, and she began to get interested in these programs —finally writing in for one of the Bible study courses they talked about. "I was getting interested in what was in this 'Word of God' they kept talking about. And I liked them—the announcers. They were sincere, but they were friendly and made jokes, and they talked about the ideas of people my own age, and they always answered the questions I sent in."

Having hardly any friends and feeling so isolated from her brothers, she found the programs began to mean a lot. "It used to do something to me when they talked about Jesus and what it was like to have a faith that worked everyday," she says. "I began to see that faith was not an abstract idea but could be practical."

From time to time she dipped into the Bible correspondence lessons they sent her, but she didn't take the course seriously until she came across words from the book of Romans one day: "What an unhappy man I am. Who will rescue me from this body that is taking me to death?" "I was startled," she says.

Then her lesson took her to Matthew 10: "For only a penny you can buy two sparrows, yet not one sparrow falls to the ground without your Father's consent. As for you, even the hairs of your head have all been counted. So do not be afraid; you are worth much more than many sparrows."

In an instant the words did something to Mamiko the Gloomy: they showed her someone cared. "The minute I read it,

---

* SINPO: Technical shorthand for quality of short wave radio reception within a target area. S: Signal, I: Interference, N: Noise (atmospheric), P: Propagation (transmission), O: Overall merit. On a scale of 5, in which 5 equals excellence.

I realized, 'This is it! There *is* someone who cares about me, not just a little bit but very much.'" She stared at the words in front of her, then prayed her first prayer: "God, if You exist, please help me. Every day I feel empty inside. Please look after me." She had barely finished the prayer when she burst into tears. "When I asked God to do this, tears poured down my cheeks," she says. But then she suddenly felt euphoric. "It suddenly seemed as if I had nothing more to worry about, and I wanted to laugh."

She didn't say much to her family. It was too risky. They were Buddhist, albeit only nominal, but Grandfather had been a good Buddhist, and her parents had met through the temple's match-making services. As a family they used to visit the temple once a year, at New Year, but the idea of someone in the family seriously adopting another religion would only alarm them. So she quietly told her mother and left it at that. Her brothers just thought she had some philosophical interest in Christianity.

But when she was fifteen, she began going to a church in Sapporo, and later, at a summer camp, she decided to commit herself. "I decided to follow God all my life." As she began to pray, she often asked for empathy with people she found difficult to like. As she read in the Bible about gentleness, she began to control her short temper. And bit by bit her embarrassment began to fade. "I began to realize that it was more important what God thought about me than what other people did." She made enough progress that she even enjoyed presiding over a debate between high school students in the church—"even though I sometimes tripped over my words or forgot what to say."

She still finds it difficult to join in her friends' conversations, but she began to see reasons why and to work on them. "I began to realize it was because I thought their talk was beneath me—and that I had to get rid of that sort of attitude. Obviously Jesus didn't think like that because He came from heaven to earth."

In 1986 Mamiko left Sapporo to start college in Tokyo. She still listens to the broadcasts and often sends copies of the short-wave schedule to her friends in Japan's growing group of radio hobbyists who send useful reception information to stations. She

feels open enough now with her family that she occasionally records a program for them.

Over a couple of years Mamiko the Gloomy has become
Mamiko the Cheerful. "I pray about everything, and my days are
full," she says. "Now no one can imagine that I used to be the
way I was. At least, that's what my friends from junior high tell
me."

9
BERMUDA TRIANGLE

Pilot Sets runs quickly through the pre-flight procedure: air intakes clear, wing and tail flaps free, engine revs OK, radio communications, gauges, and instruments all OK.

He drops lightly out of the cockpit to the tarmac. It's early at Bonaire's Flamingo Airport. The sun is just up, and the bright little Caribbean island seems to sparkle in the first light. The forecast is good. Sets is taking a party of five from Bonaire to another little island in the sun—St. Maarten—five hours away by air to the northeast, following the giant loop of the Antilles chain of islands flung across the sea like pearls on deep blue velvet.

Robert Sets is a Caucasian from St. Maarten. Bonaire and St. Maarten, 500 miles apart, are part of the Netherlands Antilles, six small Caribbean islands tossed from one proud empire to another over the last five centuries, and Papiamento shows the effects: the native language of Bonaire is a potpourri of Spanish, Portuguese, French, African, English, and Dutch.

All Sets's passengers that morning are from Bonaire except Anke Klomp, a Dutch anthropologist visiting to study the island's colonial architecture. Except for Tom Hernandez, who seems to have some Latin in him, they are all Dutch. Henk Dammerman has lived on Bonaire and done business there for years; Nol Sorée is the local bank manager, Julius Heitkonig the island's only jeweler. An interesting character is Julius—loves to care for sick animals, like flamingos with broken wings. He's even put artificial legs on a couple of the graceful birds. He also owns the only boa constrictor on the island, an indolent eight-foot snake originally from Colombia, called Timo. Timo is now housed in the "zoo" behind Heitkonig's shop.

As they squeeze into the six-seater, the mood is light. Cleared for take-off, Sets gives the Cessna full throttle, lifts her off like a feather, and flies along the island chain to St. Maarten. On St. Maarten the group inaugurates a new service club, meets with old friends, and parties into the night.

Planned departure time is 12:00 noon next day—Sunday, May 16—and to save time, Sets plans a direct route back to Bonaire across 500 miles of open sea. The weather report is for good and stable conditions, and visibility is perfect; wind speed 18 knots—normal.

Midday Sunday, Sets warms the engines and waits for clearance. At 4,000 feet he asks the control tower at St. Maarten to let Bonaire know their anticipated time of arrival—1600 hours—and everyone settles back for the four-hour flight. Sets, his eyes flicking continuously over the instruments, prepares for a routine trip. In the distance, to the east, is a towering mass of cumulus clouds—nothing out of the ordinary.

Nol Sorée sits back and mentally savors the Indonesian food he'll be eating on Bonaire that night at the governor's; a connoisseur of exotic foods, his mouth is watering already. After an hour in the air, standard fare is served: crackers, young Dutch cheese, and hot coffee from the thermos.

Sets checks the fuel gauge for the left tank: all normal. But a sudden humming and a slight steady vibration in the steering yoke worry him; he's too experienced a pilot to ignore it. It's quite distinct from the steady drumming of the engines he knows so well.

The plane shudders suddenly but settles back immediately. Sets doesn't like it at all; something isn't right. His eyes flicker over the instrument panel: height 4,000 feet; speed 160 knots—normal; engines 2,300 rpm—normal; controls—normal. He looks again at the cloud conditions. Cloud activity has increased but nothing to cause alarm. Predictions are good; the St. Maarten weather office hasn't reported any turbulence. Nothing out of the ordinary.

Then it happens. As if taken in some giant grasp the small plane is borne so powerfully upward the passengers are pinned in their seats. Up and up. Suddenly it's pitch black outside and sheets of rain cascade onto the riveted metal plates of the fuselage like volleys of rifle fire.

The passengers stare wide-eyed and uncomprehendingly at each other. They don't know it, but they are being carried up at about 9,000 feet a minute. Robert Sets, fists frozen around the steering yoke, is totally helpless at the controls; the plane won't respond. Then, as if released by the same giant hand, the small plane stops and hangs motionless in the pitch darkness. Sets takes a frantic look at the altitude gauge and can't believe his eyes—12,000 feet!

Then the little plane pitches into a crazy descent, tumbling faster and faster. Samsonite suitcases burst open, discharging their contents and catapulting around the cabin. Crackers and cups fly through the air. Tom Hernandez, who's forgotten to fasten his seat belt, is spread-eagled across the roof.

Sets realizes with horror that he's been overtaken by one of the gigantic turbulences for which the region is feared. Any pilot caught in one counts himself dead. Dimly he's also aware that he is on the perimeter of the legendary Bermuda Triangle, where aircraft and ships have been lost without a trace, their last radio communications reporting sudden bad weather and loss of orientation.

Sets looks at his compass—it's oscillating wildly. Some gauges are dead, others give impossible readings. But it's the altimeter that terrifies him: it rushes down—3,000 . . . 2,400 . . . 1,800 . . . 1,200 feet. And nothing below but angry ocean.

Then the small craft is caught upward again, as powerless as a leaf in a tempest, finally to sit motionless for an instant at 12,000 feet before plummeting madly down again. This time the sea comes closer—900 . . . 600 . . . 450 feet. Sets bites clean through his lower lip, unconscious of the pain. Through the sheets of driving rain he can see mountainous waves.

The high-pitched pulse of the automatic stall-warning beeper penetrates the frenzy, and Sets shuts his eyes. This is it —curtains! The plane is barely 200 feet above the water, with no engine speed. Any second it will stall. He braces himself for the hard impact with the ocean. But nothing happens. All he can hear is the sound of the Cessna's hard-running engines and, above it, the noise of the stall-warning beeper. Opening his eyes a slit he sees the plane is still flying—hovering rather than flying —dangerously close to the water. He can't believe it.

He pulls back on the stick, very gently, and for the first time the little plane responds. Scarcely able to breathe, his mind numb, his heart pounding, he eases the throttle back again. Once again the nose comes up. Sets begins to fly in a wide circle, and with agonizing slowness the Cessna gains height; they seem to be in an enormous low pressure zone. For half an hour, he circles . . . an hour. Slowly the cloud mass above them begins to break up, and like a miracle shafts of sunlight break through. An hour and a half later they are back at a reasonable flight altitude. The clear weather turbulence is over.

Sets, sweating and shaking, looks over his shoulder through a side window at the wings, unable to believe they're still intact. They are, but clearly rippled under the enormous stresses they were never meant to bear.

Updrafts of tropical air like the one that caught Sets's plane are known to sweep up to heights of 30,000 feet, and downdrafts can gather speed at up to 2,500 feet a minute. At upper levels the violent rainstorms become icy sleet, freezing the controls of a plane, and the dense electrical fields scramble and then damage aviation instruments. A pilot can be deprived of oxygen at the top of the funnel long enough to lose consciousness, and crashes in these conditions are more often caused by pilot unconsciousness than by mechanical failure. Amazingly, Sets and his passengers survived.

Still in a daze Sets checks his instruments but doesn't dare rely on them. 1,700 hours—they were expected in Bonaire an hour ago. Unable to trust his compass, he takes a bearing from the sun and turns the Cessna's nose south. Repeatedly he radios distress calls, but the set seems to be dead. He can't receive anything either; the antenna must have been torn off. But he keeps dialing. At the moment his communications radio is the most important instrument on board; he has to find a local radio station to be able to get the plane on course.

His brain is working again, and he weighs his chances. With his radio out, the sun is his only navigational aid. But the sun goes down at 1830 hours. He's been flying for more than an hour on the reserve tank. If he misses the island, as he probably will, he'll have to try to get all the way to Venezuela—40 miles —and he doubts he has enough fuel. Even if he makes it, the prospects of landing safely on Venezuela's dangerous coastline without instruments and in pitch tropical darkness is bad. If he ditches in the sea, at night, the chances of survival are about equal: zero.

They've survived the storm, but that's all.

Henk Dammerman sees a big oil tanker 4,000 feet below them and tries to jump out. It takes a long time to calm him; he's completely irrational.

Sets turns the radio dial once more, then stares incredulously at the small receiver. Radio communication! From the island of Bonaire itself, Trans World Radio's transmitters and the Dutch voice is clear in the silent cabin: ". . . if you hear God's call today, do not reject it. . . ." Suddenly everyone talks at once. They know the speaker—one of their island compatriots, Rev. Jan Jonkman. The signal from the 500,000 watt medium wave transmitter is so powerful that it needs no help from an antenna to reach the receiver.

The time is 1745 hours—forty-five minutes from sunset. Sets is not to know it, but this is the first program ever aired from the island in the Dutch language. One day earlier, and there would have been no signal for Sets at 1745 hours.

Holding his breath, Sets switches on the radio directional finder. It works! He fine tunes the radio to get the clearest reception on the signal from Bonaire and checks the finder's reading for distance and direction to the station . . . then shivers involuntarily. He is miles too far to the east. He would never have seen the island. He is heading straight for the lonely expanse of water between the islands and the Venezuelan coast, and he would probably have gone down in it.

Sets alters course 180 degrees to the west and homes in with the directional finder on the transmitters. Excitement turns to silence. The words of Jan Jonkman, so finely tuned, are crystal clear. ". . . This is your chance. You don't know if you will ever have another. Everyone has an opportunity in life to believe in Jesus Christ as Lord and Savior. Today, Jesus Christ is searching for the person prepared to surrender to His call. Don't ignore Him any longer. Whoever you are who are listening, don't delay any further. . . ."

The outline of Bonaire—just twenty-four miles long—is now visible. It's 1810 hours—twenty minutes from the sunset that so quickly brings darkness to the tropics. Sets can now make out the small airport, and he banks so he can come in from the west, into the prevailing wind. It's a careful visual landing and a gingerly touchdown. The undercarriage holds. Sets taxies onto the apron, shuts down the engines, and switches off the radio.

The group disembarks, shaken and quiet. It was far too close. They stop and stare at the station's giant red and white towers. Soon the regulation red lights will be switched on—they always are with the onset of darkness. Quietly they make their way home.

Later that evening, they all turn out to the governor's function, and they don't have to ask each other why they're there. After such a close call, it takes a good party to help get over the shock.

Sets was not the only pilot to use Trans World Radio's Bonaire signal as a navigational aid. Commercial aircraft pilots flying in the region are known to set their instruments by the signal as soon as they enter the Caribbean.

Sets died only a few years after the incident. Anke Klomp, after she completed her studies, returned to Holland. Julius Heitkonig and Mel Sorée were still living on Bonaire at the time of writing, but it was never obvious that the incident gave them pause for thought. A day after the incident Henk Dammerman visited Jan Jonkman and told him that for the first time in his life he had prayed as the plane was tossed like flotsam through thousands of feet. He also said that for the first time in his life he had listened while Jan Jonkman said: "You may never have another chance. Today if you hear His voice. . . ."

Kazuhiro Kamobayashi   FEBC
Japan

10
YAKUZA

The Yakuza is one of the largest criminal organizations in the world today: the Japanese version of America's Mafia, a multi-billion-dollar empire built on vice and violence, and with a clear record of political patronage.

Japanese police statistics put the number of Yakuza at about 100,000, though the total is widely believed to be higher; certainly Japanese Yakuza outnumber the American Mafia.

Not all Yakuza business is conducted underground. Yakuza run coffee houses, bars, nightclubs and cabarets, restaurants and entertainment venues, construction and trash collection companies, retail outlets, real estate firms; at least twenty-four thousand such businesses are on record. It also invests heavily in sport and leisure. But it is the Yakuza's illicit activities that bring in most of its cash—a conservatively estimated $3.8 billion in 1983 from gambling, prostitution, financial racketeering, blackmail and extortion, drugs, contraband, pornography, and sexual slavery. The Japanese Police Association estimates Yakuza illegal income at up to $8 billion, but independent estimates run as high as $22 billion.

Kazuhiro Kamobayashi was a member of the Yakuza during the seventies in Tokyo, where most Yakuza syndicates have their headquarters. As with other apprentice Yakuza, he would have spent six to twelve months at menial tasks: cooking, cleaning, answering phones, chauffeuring the boss, arranging the shoes in order. His hair would have been close-cropped, his clothes flashy.

Early on he would have learned the unwritten Yakuza rules: never reveal the secrets of the organization, never personally take drugs, never appeal to police or the law, never violate the wife or children of another member, never withhold money from the gang, never fail to obey your superiors. Gangsters a little careless about obeying orders lost the top phalange of their little finger; another misdemeanor and they lost the next joint. Kazuhiro may have had a joint or two removed—he doesn't say—but he does say that his chest and back were covered with the extraordinarily intricate and elaborate tattoos peculiar to the Yakuza. The tattoo is a badge of membership and manhood, gained over months at considerable expense, in a long series of painful jabs with a bamboo sliver. Yakuza wear their tattoos with great pride; the tattooed gangster is very serious about his commitment to the Yakuza.

Kazuhiro doesn't say how long he spent with the Yakuza; he only mentions the organization in passing. He's more interested in talking about the medium wave transmission he's just heard from FEBC's installation on the island of Cheju Do in South Korea.

His first letter arrived at FEBC offices in Japan on January 4, 1988, from Nagasaki—the industrial city on the southern island of Kyushu, which was blown apart by an American atomic bomb on August 9, 1945.

"I happened to hear you a couple of days ago when I was trying to find some good music," he writes. "As I listened to you and the beautiful hymn you played, I started to weep, and I couldn't stop. You asked listeners to write, so I am writing. I am forty-two, and I'm in a mental hospital. I want very much to forget and bury my past."

Kazuhiro says he lost his mother suddenly when he was twenty-six. He felt tortured with guilt that he had not taken better care of her. "But I was living in Tokyo, and she was far away. She spent herself just to love and raise me. Her death ruined my whole life and I became so desperate I didn't care how I lived, and it was fast and loose. I joined the Yakuza. I was ready to throw my life away for anything, at anytime. I didn't fear God or Buddha."

But he was haunted by the "great love and sadness" he last saw on his old father's face. "He was a Christian, and he used to sing hymns to me years ago. The hymn you have just played has brought it all back. I want to reform myself for my father's sake, before I die. Is it possible someone like me could be saved by trusting in Jesus Christ? I want to leave the past behind and return to God. Please help me."

The staff replied, and a month later Kazuhiro wrote again. "I felt terrible after I wrote my first letter. I thought, how could anyone like me hope to receive forgiveness? I had lived so wickedly for so long that it was too late; I could not hope to expect anything from God or others. But here I have your warm, kind letter. As I read it the tears ran down my cheeks. I said to myself, 'If I miss this chance it's the end of the road for me.' Yes, I would love to see a pastor. I am in the alcoholic ward, but I can get permission to go to town for good reason. I want to see the pastor in person, confess my sin, and find the Lord Jesus."

The staff sent Kazuhiro the gospels of Luke and John, and he wrote again a month later: "Thank you from the bottom of my heart for the two gospels. I have been reading them day and night, and I have already learned many verses by heart. I read about Jesus at the pool of Bethesda, and I heard Him command me, 'Arise, take up your bed and walk!' I heard Him say, 'You are clean through the word that I have spoken to you.' I am saved. I have decided to follow Jesus, taking up my cross daily. The pastor will see me on March 7. I am greatly looking forward to seeing him."

The pastor came. "How I wished I could have stopped the clock. God has prepared one good thing after another for me. I am so grateful. He listened to my story, and warned me that the Christian way was not easy but that it was full of blessing."

FEBC sent a New Testament and a book: "I am almost speechless. A New Testament! But isn't the Bible mysterious. You can read it over and over, and then suddenly a verse stands out, and you understand it very clearly. The pastor does not really believe you can find Christ through the radio. But that's how it happened for me. Please be my witness that I have accepted Jesus as my Lord and Savior. Your little book showed me clearly that I didn't even receive Christ by my own faith but because God was so merciful. This precious Lord has come to dwell in me. How wonderful! With all my heart I can say that I have accepted Jesus Christ who is full of life. I am so full of peace and joy. God has forgiven me, and I am clean. I have dedicated my whole life to Him and asked Him to use it."

Sometime in the midyear Kazuhiro was discharged from the psychiatric hospital and he wrote again: "Thank you so much for your faithful prayers to the Lord for me. I have been greatly blessed by God. Now—hear the great news. I have a job! The head of a newspaper distribution agency came all the way to Nagasaki from Tokyo to interview me—nothing less than a miracle. I had applied for work everywhere now, but no one would employ me because of my background. (I told them honestly that I had been a Yakuza.) But when I wrote to this company I told them that I was a Christian now, and how it happened. When Mr. Honda came he asked me which church I belonged to. I said I hadn't been to a church yet, and that FEBC was my church. I told him about your programs and how they had led me to Jesus Christ. He interviewed me for two hours, then finally he said, 'I believe what you have told me, and I want to help you start a new life.' I showed him the tattoos on my back and chest, so he knew I really had been a Yakuza. He believed me. I am so happy. God my heavenly Father answered my prayer and I will be a delivery man. I will come to see you immediately I get to Tokyo. My only regret is that I have to leave my old father here on Kyushu. I hate doing it."

Two staffers met Kazuhiro at the station and spent some time with him. They posted a snapshot of Kazuhiro to his father, who replied immediately. "Thank you so much for your kindness and for meeting my son at Tokyo station. I weep with joy as I remember how happy he was at the thought of seeing you again. His life was a wreck. I'm so glad he found your programs. Thank you so much for the photograph. I have never seen such a smile on his face, or his eyes sparkling like that."

Kazuhiro stayed in touch with staff by telephone while he was in Tokyo, but the thought of his father, aged and alone, troubled him so much that he resigned his job several months later and returned to Nagasaki where he began to attend church regularly.

Seven months later FEBC's Tokyo office received a call from Nagasaki. The caller introduced himself as Rev. Tamaoki, Kazuhiro's pastor. "I know Kazuhiro would have wanted me to call you as soon as possible," he began. "He was such a faithful worshiper, a sincere man, with deep spiritual understanding. And such a hard worker. He painted the church for us this spring, and it was such a professional job that everyone wanted to know who had done it. I want you to know he died suddenly of acute hepatitis. He never tired of telling us about you. He said he had never trusted anyone in his life until you began writing to him, and when you met him at Tokyo station you helped him begin trusting others. He was at every service; he used to bring an alcoholic friend and tried to present Christ to him every way he could. He never missed a prayer meeting."

The staff sent a sympathy card to Kazuhiro's father, and the old man replied promptly. "Thank you so much for your warm gesture of sympathy. It is such a comfort to know that Kazuhiro is with the Lord, in peace. I will never forget your kindness to him. You did so very much for us. Thank you."

Part 2

I thought all night about what you said. I felt as if someone had come to pull me out of a pit into which I was falling. I felt peaceful as I listened. I am seventeen and I heard your program by accident. I want to know more details.

TWR
Saudi Arabia

When I started listening to your programs, I decided I might as well start reading the Bible. A year later I got interested in people who practised genuine Christianity, not mere religion. One day at midnight I decided to follow Jesus Christ.

TWR
Israel

My wife and I have been helped so much by your programming. We sense the hand of God's blessing on you. All three of our children have died, so, after being married twenty years, we don't have any living with us. But we know that Christ is at the center of our home. Your programs day by day help fill us, as children of God, with peace and love.

WMBI, WMBI-FM
United States

Peking is about 3,300 miles from Sri Lanka—at least twice the reach of Trans World Radio's Sri Lanka medium wave signal. But a Bengali student studying at the School of Mines and Steel in Peking wrote saying he'd been listening regularly with several Indian friends to Trans World Radio's Bengali programs from Sri Lanka. "Impossible," radio engineers say, "but these things can happen."

TWR
China

I wanted to let you know that I am thankful for all of your broadcasts, for it is from "accidentally stumbling" onto your station during hard times that the Spirit led an awakening within me for the love and acceptance of Christ.

WRMB
Florida

I've never heard anything like your programs. I never thought a relationship with God or Jesus Christ was possible. But now my life has been changed completely.

TWR
U.S.S.R.

We felt depressed and homesick when we first arrived here two years ago. The first piece of furniture we unpacked was our stereo unit. We turned on the radio, and without changing the dial, the first thing we heard was Trans World Radio. It was great! We realized there were other Christians on the island and that God was with us.

TWR
Guam

I praise God for your ministry to me and my famiiy and all of us listening. Your signal is strong, clear, and consistent, and so is your message. I manage a cafe in . . . Washington, and we continue to have our radio tuned into the translator every day. Our hours are a little weird. We open at midnight through two in the afternoon, and there's a great number of hurting people out late at night.

KMBI
Washington state

11
A LITTLE KID AGAIN

Marwan is a tall, smooth-skinned Palestinian Arab from the West Bank. He's driven 30 kilometers south to Jerusalem from Bir Zeit University, where he's a lecturer in civil engineering, just to see you, even though he needs every moment he's got to mark student examination papers. In addition, he's stuffed up with a cold, feeling lousy, and wrapped up like a hot water bottle. He apologizes he's late: he couldn't get away, and winter's wet weather traffic slowed him down further. He speaks in English; three years at England's Cambridge University did a lot to help his fluency.

The load that dropped off him that day, Marwan says in his thoughtful, deliberate way, was the fear of eternal separation from God. He settles back into one of the deep chairs in the hotel his father manages. "I didn't realize how miserable it had made me. I was a Christian, I loved Christ, but I wasn't at all sure that I was eternally safe."

Marwan was raised in a Christian home in Jaffa, Palestine. His father was an Orthodox, his mother Roman Catholic. His parents were among thousands of Palestinians dispossessed after war ignited in 1948 between Arab and Jew over the existence of the new state of Israel. Like everyone else they thought they would be returning home when the fighting stopped, but it never did. They left hurriedly, taking only a few clothes, and never returned. They lost everything as Israel enlarged its area by half, and there was no compensation. They just had to start life again, and they did, in Arab territory north of Jerusalem, in the town of

Ramallah. Marwan's father was a jeweler and moneychanger. He reclaimed capital loaned to Lebanese and Syrian merchants and reopened the business.

But in the Six-Day War, Israel occupied the West Bank, including Ramallah, and again the family was an unwanted element. But this time they stayed put.

"My father taught us to look philosophically and forgivingly at our Jewish neighbors and to fear God," Marwan says. "At home we see it this way. In the past the Jews were the victims. Now we are. We can have friendships with them. They aren't the ones who've hurt us; it's the policy-makers."

Marwan has warm memories of family devotions when he was a child. "We used to read Bible stories together and sing hymns. I used to read the Bible every night and pray." He went to a local Roman Catholic school where he was a bright student. He also had a clear sense of duty about his responsibilities as a Christian and, in his last three years in Ramallah, headed up the school's student Christian movement.

He was seventeen and a student studying engineering in Egypt when he developed a regular Radio Monte Carlo listening habit. He liked the easy-listening music as a subdued background while he studied, and when the station closed down at 9:30 P.M. he usually left the radio on for the 10:00 P.M. Trans World Radio program on the same frequency. "But I didn't listen too closely to Trans World Radio," Marwan says. "I was already a Christian, so I figured I wouldn't learn a whole lot."

After graduation he enrolled for Ph.D. studies in engineering at Cambridge University and, as he started the study year, invested in a new radio, hoping to tune in broadcasts from near home. He never did pick up much, but in the process he discovered a Trans World Radio medium wave Arab language broadcast out of Monte Carlo to the North African nations and Europe. This time he listened, "because at that time I had questions I was wanting answers to," he says.

The questions had surfaced some time earlier, but he'd felt awkward about approaching his priest, and his Christian friends didn't know the answers. "The real question I was faced with was: What happens to me if I am in a state of sin and I die?" Marwan says. "Will I be with Christ? I was a Christian, but I could see how far away I was from the perfection of Christ. I loved the person He was, and I was unhappy I failed so often to be like Him. And little by little I had begun to think that if I died while I was failing to live up to Jesus' standards, I would die outside the forgiveness of God and wouldn't go to heaven. Salvation by God's gift and not by works was part of the doctrine in the church where I went, but it wasn't taught. A priest would tell you if you asked him, but otherwise you didn't hear it."

So as he studied at Cambridge, he listened regularly to Trans World Radio's late evening medium wave Arabic broadcasts, and as he did the matter began to clarify. When he could, he read up on the subject.

"It literally came as a revelation to me that I *was* saved, that I wasn't in and out of God's acceptance depending on what I had or hadn't done," he says. "I was saved because Christ died for me, and whether I doubted it or not made no difference. If I sinned, it was no problem. I could ask God to forgive me, and in the meantime I hadn't lost my salvation."

He sent away for a booklet advertised on one of the programs: *Salvation, Assurance, Joy.* It reinforced what he'd been hearing. "The facts didn't change just because I doubted them," he says. "I was saved because I belonged to Christ. I was saved all the time, no matter what. The effect on me was momentous . . . as if I'd dropped a heavy burden. I felt like a brand new person. I'd been so worried. It literally changed my life. . . . I was so happy. It was probably like that when I was a little kid, but little by little you start to carry your own burdens instead of casting them on Christ. But that was a time when God lifted everything off me. And when it really got hold of me, I found something interesting: it was so much easier to love people. I loved far more widely and deeply. I also found it far easier to take the humbler path."

He found something else, too. "I found some things didn't matter so much. Before, I would never let my Bible touch the floor or where people sat, because it was a holy book. But after that it really didn't matter. It was the contents that were important, not the book. I began to do more mundane things while I listened to the broadcasts . . . like wash my socks. I no longer thought of a religious broadcast as so holy that you couldn't think of socks during it."

He listened often to Trans World Radio during his three years at Cambridge University. "I don't doubt that if TWR hadn't been there, God would have used something else to show me. But it was there, so He used it." He also appreciated hearing English-language translations of the Bible because they sometimes shed new light on the Arab text.

Cambridge University has a memento in one of its chapels of the "new day" that dawned on Marwan while he was studying there. Not just an engineer but a painter in oils, he brushed onto canvas his own depiction of the Emmaus Road incident: Jesus breaking bread with two men after he had "opened the Scriptures" to them. The biblical account of the same event simply says, "Their eyes were opened and they knew Him."

12
THE COLONEL'S ARMY

The single-prop four-seater circles just on the border of Guyana and drops over the muddy river to land. The strip—or what passes as a strip—is coming up fast, then you're down, and the light plane is slewing in the red mud. Out the window a couple of squealing pigs bolt in panic.

You climb out and look around. The silence is heavy. The cloud is low; humidity is high. It's warm. The hills are dark, conical, and smooth; it's a strange, brooding landscape. The pilot looks anxiously back down the strip, already worrying how he's ever going to get out again.

You're hundreds of miles from anywhere. Brazil's northernmost town, Boa Vista, is an hour's flying time behind, and the impenetrable tropical jungle of the Brazilian interior farther back still. You've been flying over flat savannah, ranching country, but this is way out back and hilly—Indian territory. Not too many Brazilians up here, mainly those who come up to get rich quick on the gold or diamonds. The strip obviously serves a nearby group of huts—four or five thatched mud and stick houses in a bare enclosure encircled by a few trees. Two dirty children come to investigate and drape themselves over a couple of wooden bars that serve as a gate. A dog and a goat trot over.

Several of Messias's girls are already here to take you forty-five minutes through the wet growth and across a strongly running, swollen, brown river in a couple of dugouts that don't look any wider than a man could lie in. The kids bail out the water and hold the wooden canoes steady while you slither down the bank, stumble in, and crouch motionless. "Don't move once we're going," they warn. You have visions of the crocodiles getting you—the crocodiles or the piranhas or the water snakes —and all the cassette tapes and notes going to the bottom. What a waste. They shove off against the current out to center stream, then let the current sweep the two canoes over to the landing point on the other side. Huh! Uneventful!

Light rain starts to fall, and you make sure the tape-recorder is on the underside of the pack and well protected in plastic. You start finding out about Messias and the area as you trudge through tall wet scrub that seems trackless—*how do these kids ever remember the way?* There are a lot of minerals in "them thar hills," the translator says—diamonds, uranium, gold, iron ore. The translator's been here before—knows Messias and that's good, because that way Messias will talk more.

Messias runs one hundred eighty head of cattle up here, as well as sheep and goats. He's also turned the dark, fertile soil into a vegetable and fruit farm that's better than anything else for hundreds of miles. He feeds his family off it, and half the neighbors. You mean there *are* neighbors out here? "Yep, here and there, but you have to walk a bit to find them. Nearest village is three hours away." Messias is also a diamond miner; he's sluiced away whole hills in his forty-three years up here.

To the right the airstrip that would have avoided this walk is coming into view. No wonder the pilot wasn't game. It runs uphill at a 17° angle. The place is a burial ground for light planes, the translator says casually . . . for one reason or another: unsafe planes, bad weather, lack of flying experience.

You round a bend and follow the river. Somewhere in a grove of trees are Messias and his twelve daughters.

"How come he's got no sons?"

"Why don't you ask him?"

"I will."

Suddenly you've arrived: a big, clean, white-washed, mud-brick house with a thickly thatched roof of palm leaves that bush well out over the walls. The property is densely planted with flowering plants, each bordered with tin cans driven into the ground to stop the household menagerie scratching at the roots.

There's a stir inside. You've been told the girls get up early and spend the whole morning pressing their clothes if they think a family photo's going to be taken. But as they appear it's obvious they aren't expecting pictures; they look like cowgirls, the lot of them: blue denims, tee-shirts, ten-gallon hats, and wide grins. And cowgirls they are—they can rope and throw and brand a steer as good as any Texan.

Messias appears, trousers rolled up to mid-calf and shirt hanging out. He's slight but looks tough and wiry. He's going gray late, and he's kept his hair; he looks fifty-five. He wears glasses and looks intelligent. They say he's pretty sharp—would have made a good lawyer with a bit of education—and witty.

You step inside, and judging by the activity and noise somewhere through the wall, hot dinner is being prepared. Messias is a bit on guard, isn't sure why you want to make him a chapter in a book. But he explains he came here forty-three years ago from Brazil's poor northeast. He was illiterate, still is, and from a big family. He was the only one who wanted to head into the gold country, get rich quick, then go back and live like a king. But he never got rich. He was twenty-four when he got here. You do a bit of mental arithmetic: *Twenty-four plus forty-three—he can't be sixty-seven! Must be. Life out here keeps 'em young.*

He's not saying a whole lot; he needs some time to warm up—maybe after dinner, or if we get him talking about his girls. "How old's the oldest, and how young's the youngest?" you suggest helpfully. The translator obliges. Messias looks perplexed, "Now you've asked a hard one. We've got it in a notebook somewhere." He gets their names muddled too; teen-agers all look alike, he says. True, but there aren't many teen-agers left now; seven of them are in their twenties. They must have arrived one after the other in the first ten years. How on earth did their mother cope? They say she's a hard worker, his little Macuxi Indian wife, all dressed up today in her best brown frock. But the whole family apparently works like Trojans.

Messias calls for a family roundup, and someone shoots off to get the missing members. The girls start trooping in at namecall, and Messias tells them to give their ages and explain their responsibilities.

First up is Ivonne, thirty. Maria Auxiliadora, twenty-nine, isn't here; she's married and studying at a Bible college in the far south. Vanda is twenty-eight, Maria Costa twenty-seven, also married with a little boy called—wait for it—Billy Graham. Ivette is twenty-five, Rozinete twenty-three, Imperatriz twenty-one, named after a city. Marli is nineteen, Francisca seventeen, Vanderleia sixteen, Aldermora fourteen, and Tiani Cristina eight. Their duties are wide and wondrous. Messias runs his household like a colonel runs a crack regiment. They're awake at 4:30 A.M., and they work till 4:00 in the afternoon. They know exactly what they have to do, and they do it.

Ivonne is the cook. Vanda makes clothes for the rest of the household and works the diamond mine. Ivette is a cattle rancher, diamond miner, and medical attendant—later they're going to show you the clinic that operates from the house. Rozinete, also a medical attendant, takes care of the menagerie—pigs, ducks, chickens, turkeys, goats, and dogs, and works in the fields and the vegetable garden, both of which seem to produce prolifically: lettuce, onions, beans, corn, rice, pumpkin, gherkin, carrots, peas, tomato, cassava, avocado, sweet potato, cabbage. And that doesn't include the fruit orchard: lemon, orange, tangerine, mango, pineapple, melon, banana, sugar cane. (No wonder they all look so healthy!) The march-past continues: Imperatriz—cattle, mine, fields, and garden; Marli—fields, cattle, and mine; Francisca—sheep and mother's help in the flower garden and local household vegetable plot; Vanderleia—flower garden, and sheep; Aldemora—kitchen helper and household cleaner, tidier, and maintenance woman. Tiani helps with the calves and cattle, and waters the plants.

The parade and explanations have taken thirty minutes. The duties circulate, and depending on the season, it can be all hands to the mine or all hands to the fields. The wet season is the time to work the mine; the copious rainfall helps in the sluicing. Planting and harvesting need an army. What does looking after the livestock entail? Well, first of all, locating them on this rambling 4,900-acre property, rounding up, castrating, branding, dosing, delivering, killing for meat. The girls are as at home on horses as they are on their own two feet. You learn with some amazement that they also built the house: cut the poles miles away and carried them over the mountains, made their own brick from special clays, which they also had to dig out and carry, laid the concrete floor, plastered, painted, and decorated. No wonder this family has a reputation!

Messias is beginning to open up but not about his origins. Some suspect he killed a man and fled. It was common enough in this region. Messias says only that he was "terrible, violent, and destructive," and is amazed he survived. No one can get him to talk about the time when he was a Communist and Communism was outlawed by the military government, but it's got around that he changed the names of his kids when he became a believer: one of them used to be called Havana, another Indo-China. He doesn't say, but it's well enough known that he used to listen a lot to Cuba's Radio Havana up here—the signal came in loud and clear.

The meal is served: chicken, rice, beans, eggs, lettuce, lemon—all off the property. The water comes from the stream below the house. The table only seats four or five people; the kids fill up their enamel plates and plant themselves round about to listen.

Messias walked the couple of hundred miles out here from Boa Vista, alone, unarmed, and relying on the local Indians to feed him. He was young, seeking his fortune, and just one of many. In the rough mining settlement he drank, womanized, gambled, and got in brawls and knife and gun fights over cards, gold, and diamonds, especially after he'd had too much Cachaca. He remembers when he pulled a knife on a card-sharp who had the advantage. "If he had reacted I would have killed him," he says. "That's what I was like." It was this incident that made him sit up and think. He'd almost killed a man over a card game. He figured that drinking and gambling led to uncontrollable anger and violence and that violence never led anywhere productive. He was living—maybe married at the time—with a local Indian woman, with about five kids under the age of six years. He began laying off the drinking and gambling, and the womanizing, then the tobacco.

The reform was already under way when he first heard Trans World Radio. The signal sailed in as clearly as Radio Havana's. Messias had no religious background, and he was suspicious because he'd found the world was full of liars; he lied himself. But for some reason he believed that what he heard was true. He listened to explanations of what the Bible was about, heard he was a sinner—he didn't doubt it—listened to personal advice to listeners who'd written in, and thought it was different and good; heard stories of people a bit like himself—criminals, killers, thieves—who'd changed dramatically.

It was the stories that made him switch on the radio time and time again. And he liked the songs they sang. It was all so different from the life he knew. He couldn't help feeling that God must have kept him alive for a reason, because he should have been dead by now—violently. He listened for two years, becoming more and more convinced he needed to do something about it. When they talked one day about the cross of Christ, and His death for the sins of the world, he felt a "huge load" lift off. He felt a serenity he'd never had before and that he couldn't explain, but he wasn't sure he'd done it right. When he heard a missionary was to visit the area he went to see him and plied him with questions. The missionary reinforced what he'd heard and filled in a few gaps. Messias returned home satisfied.

And that's when Messias's household began to convert. It wasn't just Messias who listened, but his little Mucuxi wife and the kids—and there were more kids to come, another six or so. Messias couldn't read, so the kids taught each other how to read the Bible. Maria Auxiliadora was bright; she picked up enough during her four months in school to teach herself how to read, and then she taught the others. There was no church for miles —"hours" is the word they use out here—so Trans World Radio became their church. They also began holding Sunday services in their own home, the kids taking it in turns to be preacher.

Missionaries based in Boa Vista learned of Messias's change of heart and began working with him. Messias's house became a base for a joint state-missionary medical clinic to the area. It dispensed the essentials: snake venom medicine, painkillers and antidotes for malaria, medicines for dysentery, worms, and amoeba. The kids go out with medicines on horseback journeys of up to three or four days, treating the sick up to fifty miles away, chatting about their faith at the same time and telling people to listen to Trans World Radio. Their missions of mercy take them away seven or eight times a month.

People up to three hundred miles around have got to know Messias and his girls very well. They're so different. While most of his neighbors live in basic one or two room huts of mud and sticks, keeping a few chickens and cattle, growing a few staple crops and fishing from the rivers, Messias is living like a king on the work of his hands and those of his tribe of daughters. The house is large and immaculately clean and tidy. He uses his ingenuity to develop what he's got; he's managed to produce a seedless orange by selective breeding. He makes his own coffee, and they drink it constantly—tastes like pure caffeine. He makes clear streaming molasses from his sugar cane.

"Interesting thing," Messias observes. "After I became a believer, I got a lot more productivity for no extra work." But he's not selfish. He produces far more than the family can digest, so he sells it to his neighbors, and everyone knows the prices are the best around and that Messias won't weigh them short. They give him the borax because he's got religion, and some have rumored that Messias is in league with the Americans and all his nice talk is only to get his hands on their diamonds. But they have to hand it to him; he's a better man than he was.

Messias says he still has to fight the urge to react strongly and violently when he's crossed. He considers he won a major battle when he learned to forgive. He had a chance to do it just the other day over a property battle. Rather than fight, Messias backed off and let the antagonist take title to what Messias knew was his land. But he's still struggling to forgive him, and as his face begins to color up, it's clear he wants to change the subject.

You look around the house: four bedrooms—two for their numerous guests, and two for the fourteen of them. Hammocks are slung from wall to wall. There's no electricity; the oven is made of sandstone with a perforated metal sheet passing through the center. Underneath they burn wood, and on top the food cooks slowly for hours. Their running water is the stream below; they wash in it after work and carry it up for household purposes. Brightly scrubbed pots and pans hang on the walls. Around the back, in a separate room, is the clinic, well stocked with medications. A lot of miners and locals visit for medicines. It's also the radio room; they have a good radio-telephone link to Boa Vista.

Someone says the day literally opens and closes with Trans World Radio. While it's still dark someone silently leaves a hammock and turns on the radio. It's about 4:30 A.M., a common enough rising hour in north Brazil. No one else moves. If they aren't awake they'll wake up soon enough. Then it comes, shattering the silence! Outside, the sleeping menagerie hardly stirs, it's got used to the racket, but visiting guests are jolted bolt upright and wide awake. "I sat up in bed in sheer disbelief," a missionary says later. "I was sleeping on one side of the wall, and the radio was on the other. And it was blasting, I mean blasting. You could have heard it hours away." But still no one moves. This is the pattern. Everyone lies listening for two hours—until the programs finish, then movement starts. Breakfast is 6:30 to 7:00 A.M.—perhaps ground corn cakes or porridge. Then the day starts . . . . and it winds up round the same radio with the 7:00 to 7:45 P.M. block of programs. They talk a while then hit their hammocks—until 4:30 next morning.

The girls don't listen to much else, said a programmer who visited. They kept him up till about 2:00 A.M. singing radio songs and talking, probably with mixed motives; he was young and single. "They tell you what they like about the programs, and what they don't like they don't mention," he said. The girls often write into the station asking for a birthday wish to be read, a song to be sung, or saying they enjoyed something.

The whole family gathers for "church" on Sunday, and almost always some local is staying over. He hasn't a chance: radio morning and evening, songs all day, and sermons on Sunday.

The weather's cleared a lot, and you're to see the diamond mine. Out through the flowering plants, past a scarlet bougainvillea arching over the gate, to the corral where the girls rope and throw the steers, then a ten-minute walk. The evidence of years of work is everywhere: whole hills removed by water diversion, sluicing, and sifting. No big machines out here—just a little wooden sluice-box, a couple of picks, a shovel, a hose, and twelve girls and Dad all taking turns. He shows you a valve—a plug device of straw and rocks—he's installed for varying water pressure in a diversion channel he's dug. It's industrial diamonds he gets out of this red-yellow dirt. His daughters sell them at Boa Vista—the ones who know how to read and how to read the market. It's not very lucrative. "I'd never make a living if I had to depend on diamonds," Messias says. Messias uses his diamond money to buy only what he can't produce himself. Other miners use their diamond income to buy food. "So they're no further ahead," he says.

He's trotting along the path by the stream, his shovel over his shoulder. Now's the time. "How come it's all girls, no boys?" you ask. There's no doubt Messias hears the question, but he doesn't answer. The translator looks back at you, grins, and shrugs.

Most Indian girls around here are married by the age of twenty, and usually earlier. What are they going to do about husbands? The translator doesn't ask, just explains. Most of them are sharp kids, capable, literate, and stable. They'll pick up husbands somewhere other than out here—probably in one of the cities—as Maria Auxiliadora did. Maria will be coming back in two months, after five years away, to work with the Macuxi. They plan a big homecoming, and no doubt Messias will commandeer her growing son into his workforce.

The kids are straggling out behind and in front. They're singing—they're always singing—tunes they hear over Trans World Radio. People say they always sing while they work.

You're back at the house, and the pilot is anxious about the flight back. He doesn't think he'll be able to lift off with three people aboard and the ground so soft. He wants to try it solo, then, if he gets up, fly around to a drier strip to meet you.

It's time for the family photo, and everyone bunches up and poses outside. His little Indian wife, Almeida, like Messias, is very proud of her brood. She's been a bit out of the picture, her eyes glistening with tears sometimes, because she's been so busy, and Messias's Portuguese isn't her native tongue. But as you leave she comes and presses some money into your hand—about

$2.25 American—not a lot to a North American but a sizable gift from a little Indian woman. "For Trans World Radio," the translator says. It took Almeida a lot longer to be sure about what she believes than Messias. When she was young, she was told she would never go to heaven because she couldn't read, and she was desperately sad. It was years before a missionary told her differently.

It's good-byes all around, then post-haste to a drier landing strip, this time by aluminum motorboat along a bloated brown river, and a fidgety wait for the sound of airplane engines. You're beginning to wonder if he's become another casualty when you hear the buzz, then see the plane. Visibly releasing nervous tension, the pilot bellows that he would have crashed with extra weight aboard. The four-seater was roaring at full throttle, and spitting mud everywhere when it finally lifted off near the end of the strip.

It's near dusk as you reach Boa Vista, just inside the airport's curfew regulations for light planes. In an hour's time, you think as the pilot taxis toward the hangars, Messias and his tribe of daughters will be turning on the evening program.

13
"SAFEDOOR" . . . ?

It's been a very tiring Wednesday: six screaming, celebrating kids in a small city apartment all afternoon on a rainy September day in 1980. By the time Magda sends them all home, her head is splitting. She cleans up, prepares the last few things for her son's early morning departure for a three-month health cure by the sea, and falls into bed.

But she's overtired. Sleep refuses to come. She reaches for the radio and ten to fifteen minutes of something soothing to help her drop off. She's on the verge of sleep, half aware that the program she's listening to isn't the one she first thought, when a strange word penetrates her sleepy drift. "Safedoor?" she finally mutters to herself. "What's a Safedoor?" She struggles back to consciousness. It was an English program, a religious one. Magda's mother tongue is Flemish, but her English language teacher at school was ruthless, so her English is pretty good. But this word *Safedoor?* Thoroughly awake now, she listens to the rest of the program. But the word isn't mentioned again. She switches off and lies in the darkness, and the word returns to plague her like a persistent mosquito. Finally she gets up and rummages for her Dutch-English dictionary. No such word! She scans words in the same column looking for something that sounds similar and finally finds one that makes a bit more sense—Savior. "Savior," she repeated slowly to herself. She climbs back into bed and pulls up the covers and sometime later that night falls asleep.

In the couple of days that followed, the two words chased each other around her head: Safedoor, Savior. She told Herbert about it, but he wasn't much interested. Herbert was her closest friend after her divorce several years earlier. The next Wednesday she tuned in again. It was all very different from what she knew about the church—especially the way they talked about Jesus Christ, as if He was someone they knew well. Her only concept of Jesus was of some historic figure—like Napoleon—someone who lived a long time ago, someone in the church calendar who was born at Christmas and died at Easter.

Magda still lives in the center of Antwerp, Belgium, with her son, Eddie, and her mother. Herbert is no longer in the picture. The division between them that the two words caused finished the relationship; Herbert thought Magda was taking things to extremes. But Magda liked what she was hearing, and she wanted to hear more, though she wasn't sure what it was she was liking or why. The whole thing needed a closer look. But as she kept listening, her old fear of the Bible returned. She was only a kid in school when the priest in charge of religion classes had personally warned her that the Bible was not a book she was meant to read. And he had warned her parents, too.

Magda is sitting across the table in her modest two-story apartment. Eddie is trying to keep himself quiet with a board game.

"So I was afraid of the Bible," says Magda, "and the radio often quoted from it. Often I was so afraid that I would turn the radio off in the middle of a program. But I kept listening because my desire to know more was greater than my fear." One night, after the program ended, she prayed for the first time in fifteen years—the Lord's Prayer—but this time the words meant something. In spite of her fear she decided to buy a Bible, but they were priced beyond the reach of a modestly-paid government clerk and solo mother. But the chaplain at work found her one, and when she began reading it, Herbert broke off the relationship.

Eight weeks later she tuned into a program that seemed to be talking to her alone. "At the end I was convinced that I had to ask the Lord Jesus to become my Savior, but I didn't know how to do it," Magda says. "I could see that I had sinned, and I

could see that Jesus was the Man God had sent to take the punishment for everyone's wrongdoing, and mine too. I thought
about it for two days, and then finally I couldn't ignore that inside feeling any longer. So I knelt down."

Her diary records the prayer she said that night. "Lord, I
know that my whole life is wrong. I am living for myself, and it is
wrong not to give You the attention You should have and I want
to change this. . . . You are the only one who can do this. Lord,
please forgive my disobedience and my selfishness, change me
like You want me to be and please, Lord, will You be my Savior?"

A gentle dew of quietness seemed to settle on her as she finished her prayer. "As if I had said yes to someone who had been
asking me for a long time," Magda says. And she noticed something else, too. "My fear of the Bible just went! Now that's a
strange thing. I actually *wanted* to read the Bible."

Magda didn't waste any time. She began immediately, at
1:00 A.M., at Genesis and was still going at 5:00 A.M. But doubts
remained. Had anything really happened in response to her
prayer? Should she really be reading the Bible? And what about
the conflicts between what she had been taught as a child and
what she was now reading and hearing. She wanted to go to a
church but didn't know where to go; the different denominations
and cults bewildered her. There was no one she felt able to talk
to. For nine months her only counselor was the radio. But week
by week Jesus Christ was more real, and the Bible was slowly beginning to make sense.

She went to several churches but didn't feel at home. She
also had a feeling that in time God would lead her to the right
church, so she waited, and in the meantime wrote to the broadcasters. Then she heard that an English denomination she liked
planned to set up in Antwerp. "They were people who believed
the truth and practiced it, and they loved each other—something I didn't find in many churches," Magda says. She is now
involved in setting up the church and translating into Flemish
from English small booklets explaining salvation, which she ad-
vertises for sale in the city newspapers.

Eddie is fidgeting at the table and wants to say something. He is fifteen and also a regular listener. He says he has also decided to be a Christian and wants to work for Trans World Radio. You look at him skeptically, but he says he means it.

Life has changed a lot for Magda since she first heard the programs. She has changed a lot too: less dogmatic and domineering than she used to be. And she's happier—a lot happier than she ever was before she found her "Safedoor."

14
MOSCOW: SINPO 45444

High in the earth's upper atmosphere the sun's rays interact with a thin layer of air molecules, wrenching away electrons so that they float free.

Fifty kilometers below, a shortwave radio signal, pulsating 9.5 million times a second, leaves a 100 kilowatt transmitter 2,500 feet above Monte Carlo, travels at the speed of light, refracts from the floating electrons, and speeds down toward the Soviet Union, west of the Ural Mountains.

In central Moscow, 1,400 miles from Monte Carlo in a small apartment in a nondescript tenement block, Igor tunes his heavy, old Russian-made 20-tube receiver. He's expecting the transmission. He selects the 31 meter band and dials the frequency—9515 kHz. He registers and fine-tunes the signal—to an accuracy of 300 hertz—listens a while, grimaces slightly, and takes a clean sheet of paper.

"Greetings, Nik," he scribbles in Russian. "November 16, 1985—1625 hours on 9515 kHz—*Christ and the Children* and *Word of Life*. SINPO: Signal 4, interference 3, overall merit 3." On a scale where 5 equals excellence, Igor's SINPO readout shows reception was only fair in Moscow that afternoon.

It will be some time before the letter reaches Monte Carlo through a buffer address in an East European country. But when it does it will be valuable information to staff engineers in Monte Carlo who will begin looking for another less-troubled frequency on the crowded 31 meter band. If Igor's letters keep getting through, he's going to be a useful data source in the task of selecting frequencies for broadcasts into the U.S.S.R., where homegrown religious broadcasts are illegal.

Even before *glasnost*, Igor's letter dossier was thick—one of the thickest in Monte Carlo's Russian correspondence files. It was something of a phenomenon. Far more commonly, listeners wrote in vain. Occasionally a plaintive letter would arrive: "This is my 18th letter," or "my 31st. Didn't you get any of my other ones?" Staff hadn't. Those were the unlucky ones. Others were more fortunate, but the vast majority of the U.S.S.R.'s millions of listeners to the station's thirty-eight hours of programming each week simply preferred not to take the risks of writing. But since *glasnost* became official in 1987, the trickle of letters has become a stream.

When Igor first started writing in 1985—before the Kremlin was even thinking about *glasnost*—he was very careful. Letter number one arrived at the Monte Carlo box number ostensibly from a German staying at one of Moscow's swept-up tourist hotels. There was no such German tourist, but Moscow's postal clerks were under orders to expedite mail from tourists staying at Moscow's luxury hotels. Another left Igor with a Pole returning home and a false return address on the back. In Poland the courier sent the letter on. "Ignore the return address," Igor wrote inside. "I just plucked it out of the air." But most of Igor's letters arrived through a private address in East Europe to which he also asked the radio team to address all letters. "Note it down somewhere now, so I don't have to give it to you again," he wrote early on.

He was slow to open up. His third letter gives only the barest personal particulars. "I'm 31. I got married in 1976. My wife's name is Irina; she's 26. We have a daughter, Tanya, who has just turned six. We live in a two-roomed apartment, and that's about all."

But as his letters continue to get through, bringing replies from Monte Carlo, he becomes more chatty. "I read about your travels with interest," he writes back to one of the programmers who had described a family trip through West Europe. "It's just like a fairy tale. You go from one country through another, to sleep in a third, and have lunch in a fourth. From your window in Monaco you see not only France but Italy as well. From my window I can also see something—the wall of the building next door. But if I stretch a bit I can see the school where I used to go many moons ago."

It's more than a year before he tentatively mentions religion, and fifteen months before he talks about his personal beliefs.

Only after his letters have been arriving safely at Monte Carlo for eighteen months does Igor finally risk putting his private return address on a letter—his fifteenth. Until then his home address has only been a red ink dot on page fourteen of a Moscow street map he plans to send out to the Russian radio team. Even then it marks only the rough vicinity of his block. "This is to see if our postal system is actually working under the Big Change," he writes in that fifteenth letter, and he underlines the word *Change.*

A lot has become clear about Igor through his letters, but much is still unclear. His job is security sensitive. In 1987 his East European go-between—a personal friend—was unable to visit Igor in his Moscow apartment because the KGB refused to give Igor security clearance, and permission was expected to be denied for Igor to visit him in East Europe. Igor himself says only that he works in a factory, sometimes on an 11:00 P.M. to 5:00 A.M. shift. But he is a high-income earner in Soviet terms, bringing home a salary relative to an engineer's in the United States.

A black and white photograph of Igor wearing headphones at his big, metal, vintage receiver arrives after fifteen months. "This is my radio corner," he writes. "You can see what I have; it has 12 Short Wave bands and covers the frequencies from 1,500 Hz to 27 kHz. I bought it second-hand; it's very heavy, it weighs 100 kg." It looks military. "My dream is something smaller: a transistorized radio with a direct frequency read-out—one which I could take on holiday with me. I've seen some of them in a Moscow used-radio store. With the Japanese Sony ICF 2001 you just punch in the frequency you want. But it costs 900 rubles.

That's more than I can afford because I get not quite 200 rubles a month."

The photograph shows Igor sitting in front of his set, grinning widely and twisting to face the camera. He's wearing dark corduroys and a light sweater, his hair short and dark, eyebrows level over alert eyes. His left arm rests on the small sturdy table supporting the receiver, and a well-thumbed *World Radio TV Handbook* lies on the table corner. In the background are floral wallpaper and curtains printed in child's motif.

Igor is a "DXer"—a radio hobbyist exploring the ionosphere for international radio signals, sending useful reception information into stations and collecting souvenirs: QSL (report received) cards, station pennants, and insignia. Which was how Monte Carlo first got to know Igor.

On a DX Club form with the letterhead, Radio Berlin International, The Voice of the German Democratic Republic (East Germany), he wrote that he had listened at 0525 hours on June 30, 1985, to "Hour of Decision." He gave the signal a poor rating. No wonder, staff said. He had picked up an English-language program meant for English-speaking audiences in Europe and Britain.

He wrote again three months later—the letter from the Moscow Hotel. This time he'd tuned into the Russian-language version of the same program, and the rating was good. "Sept 8, 1620-1705 hours on 9495 kHz. SINPO rating 45444. Please send me a Monte Carlo QSL card. If you are interested I could regularly send you detailed SINPO information." Staff were very interested.

Next time, November 1985, Igor's report was of practical use. "On 9515 kHz you're very close to Radio Liberty (West Germany), and Radio Liberty is so heavily jammed here at the moment that it's affecting your frequency. Right now we can't hear you well at all. On 9510 kHz Algeria is broadcasting into Western Europe, but the signal in Moscow is very weak."

Monte Carlo engineers acted on the information, and two months later Igor wrote again: "I see you've changed from 9515 kHz to 9495 kHz . . . a very good choice. Now reception is very good. I was going to suggest this very frequency."

After a year of safe communication, Igor feels able to mention the subject of religion. "I guess it's been bugging you a bit," he writes in his seventh letter, "do I believe in God or not? I'll tell you straight. Yes. I would like to get a Bible, but don't know how to." Staff decide immediately to send in a Bible with a private traveler. "I like the songs you use . . . " he adds, "especially that one, 'My eyes are full of sorrow, listen people to the quiet voice of your conscience.'"

Then some useful information arrived: "I suggest you move off 11735 kHz at 1755 hours as fast as possible, because some station from the Orient, I think Radio Pakistan, is using it. At 1830 hours Radio Sofia from Bulgaria also uses it for its English language programs. Your Russian programs aren't coming through at all. I suggest you try 11690 kHz."

But before Monte Carlo staff received the letter, Igor telephoned from Moscow—the first call on record from a Russian listener. "The afternoon transmission is bad," he said after introductions all around and chitchat about his wife, Irina, and the weather. "Why don't you try 11690 kHz." Radio engineers immediately called a Finnish monitor and confirmed the interference. A frequency adjustment was made the following day, close to Igor's suggested 11690 kHz.

He wrote again: "11695 kHz is a lot better. . . . I was very happy to talk to you. My telephone call cost 18 rubles: two days' wages. You said you were so surprised that I would call, but you see, I did. I like new ways of getting acquainted." Then a few questions: "Is there a border between France and Monaco? Do you have border guards?" and a yawn, "It's 2300 hours and time to switch you on again for the last half hour of transmission on 9495 kHz. Then to bed."

On July 3, 1986, his wife, Irina, wrote for the first time. "Thank you very much for your beautiful program and songs. Igor and I agree with what you said, 'You can't stop the birds flying round your head but you can stop them nesting in your hair.' We're going to try to let only the good thoughts rest. Thank you so very much for your offer of some French perfumes. Here we can only dream about them."

July 24, 1986: A good report. "All four programs have been coming in loud and clear for the past three months. Please play again soon that song that goes, 'The cold is past, the summer has arrived . . . ' I really liked it." And some more questions: "Do you use French francs in Monaco or your own currency? One interesting thing about Monaco, you can tell whether the Prince is in the Palace by whether the flag is up or down."

September 15, 1986: "Thank you for playing the song, 'The cold is past . . . ' You said the song didn't fit the season because the cold wasn't past, it was just coming, but I would like to say that I don't think the song has much to do with the weather. I think cold describes the condition of a soul that hasn't found any room for Jesus Christ. But for the person who has, summer has come, figuratively speaking. I think it's the kind of song you can listen to when it's minus 40 degrees outside but summer in your soul.

"You know, I used to think quite a bit about where life came from, and everything around us. Finally I put it all on a shelf called Nature's Imponderables. I couldn't believe that a supernatural force—like God—was responsible. As well, Christians seemed to me to be a thoroughly unremarkable lot, and timid, as if they were always frightened of something.

"As I said, I've been DXing since 1969. On March 8, 1984, I accidentally tuned in to a Christian radio station, KFBS. Someone was talking, and what they said was absolutely riveting. I literally held my breath. At the end there was an invitation to all the listeners to kneel down by the set and ask Jesus to be their own Savior, and to do it then and there. Nik, after I did this, I felt that Christ, physically, literally, entered into my soul.

"After this, I listened some more to KFBS and then I began to hear your programs and get acquainted with you through our letters. In the two and a half years since March 8, 1984, you have helped settle the question once and for all: I am convinced now that God exists. It is just as unthinkable now for me to say that life just happened, as it once was for me to say that God created it. God made every living thing, in spite of what they told me at school and still try to feed me every day through magazines and newspapers. You also showed me that Christians are not all quiet, timid types.

"Of course, this change took time, but that's what you'd expect. You can't hope to change years of thinking in five minutes.

"Now, Nik, how do I find a personal relationship with God? Is it through prayer? Tell me how it happened with you."

Then he closes, commenting that the Bible has still not arrived after four months and that the first snow of the season has fallen. Tanya has just started school, and the just-ended vacation has left them running low on cash. The telephone call to Monte Carlo seems ages in the past. He makes a promise to test the suitability of frequencies planned for the fall broadcasts and closes in capital letters: "MAY GOD GUIDE YOU."

October 8, 1986: "The proposed Fall frequencies are good, except for a bit of nagging from Radio Pakistan on 6230 kHz at 2110 hours." He asks if Monte Carlo staff can get him a 1987 edition of *World Radio TV Handbook*, an indispensable manual for DXers, and apologizes for asking. His copy is seven years outdated, and they are not available in Moscow. A copy sent from the U.S.A. in 1984 never arrived. He mentions he is reserving the largest space on the wall in his radio corner for a station pennant and closes, "Greetings to you all from my dear wife and me. May God guard you. This month it is one year from the time we got to know each other."

Staff decided to call Igor, partly to make sure he was still "at liberty." He was. "I've received your gift," he said brightly. No one mentioned the word *Bible*.

January 1987: He was overjoyed that the *World Radio TV Handbook* had been ordered. "How can I ever thank you enough!" He has tried to find a Russian record that the staff want for broadcast but can't locate it anywhere. "I'm so sorry." A special week of evangelism to Russian audiences had sounded good in Moscow: "the reception was clear on both 6230 kHz and 7350 kHz, though 7350 kHz was a little bit weaker. I telephoned the studio on the last day just to encourage you, but you weren't there."

He says he is studying the Bible, but very slowly. "There's a lot I don't understand and I don't want to rush it." Winter has come: "temperatures are down to minus 30°C and only five degrees warmer during the day." They plan a family vacation for two weeks at a ski resort thirty miles out of Moscow, and Igor intends to take his VEF Spidola 232 (radio)—"so I don't lose touch with the outside world." It turned out Igor had more use than he'd ever imagined for his solid Latvian-made VEF Spidola. Glacial temperatures descended on Europe, and he was snowed in for the entire two weeks.

In March 1987 he crowed: "*Glasnost* is working! The winds of change have reached our postal system. For the first time I'm getting DX mail from Italy, Austria, and the U.S.A.!"

Igor still writes to the Russian radio staff and will no doubt continue to do so—encouraged by the new religious freedoms being permitted under *glasnost*. Probably, before too long, someone on the Russian radio team will meet Igor personally. In any case, his letters and phone calls have already turned him into flesh and blood—a "real" listener, not just one of the anonymous millions who for so long have been "out there somewhere" regularly tuning in the 250-plus hours a week of foreign Christian broadcasts into Russia but unable to make much in the way of response.

But the tide has been turning in Russia and is still turning. If the movement continues, it is not too much to expect that radio will be a key collaborator in a genuine religious awakening among Russia's 290 million people, who for seventy years have known only the cruel, unrelenting pressure of official atheism.

15
CAST OFF

Kuta crouched with his sister behind the rows of corn, his heart pounding. He stared at Sunali, panic in his eyes.

In the brief, tropical dusk, heavy with the fragrant scent of frangipani, the voice of Abdullah, his younger brother, was loud and swaggering, and there was no time to act, not even to turn off the radio. Only to crouch motionless, and hope fervently that they wouldn't be discovered.

"Ha, what are you two up to? Smells like a dead fish to me!" Abdullah's voice rang with the pride of his newly acquired manhood. "Here it is," he called to his friends, and snatched up the radio, looking triumphantly at Kuta. He pressed it against his ear as the group of neighborhood boys clustered round. Then his eyes widened with incredulity, and his face twisted in a sneer. "Listen to this!" he jeered and turned up the volume. One by one the boys echoed him, and Kuta swallowed hard as the taunting group headed back to the stone house on the plantation. He could only follow, Sunali gulping with fear behind him.

The jabbering group brought his father to the door—a tall, lean figure whose head just cleared the thatched roof. "Sons of demons," he shouted, "shut up, all of you!" The group scattered as his father strode over; no one got in the way of Abdullah's father. He pushed Abdullah aside as he seized the radio. "Who had the radio?" His voice jabbed the darkness. Abdullah blinked nervously as he backed away from his father and pointed at Kuta. "He did."

Kuta felt the blood drain from his face. He had always been a small boy, and thin. He had suffered through the ritual initiation to manhood only a little before Abdullah. Torn from his mother's arms and the world of women, where he had been dressed like a girl all his life, and worn his hair long, and where his father had come and played teasingly with him, he now had to cut his hair short and wear men's clothes.

Now he was to be constantly abused by his father—like all other sons his age were by their fathers. He had to obey him without question, no matter how unreasonable his demands— trailing desperately behind him all day, half running to keep up with his long stride as he paced the rubber plantation supervising his workers. As a small boy, he now had to work grueling hours. And slowly, painfully, he would earn the respect of the other men on the rubber plantation, to whom kindness was weakness, and who laughed at him, the "little man" still soft from his mother's tender care.

He remembered the day his father had come to the women's quarters demanding Kuta. He had hidden behind his mother's long skirts while she had answered his father. "Patience, you don't need him yet. He's so small. Let him stay with me a while yet. Away with you." Brave words, but the legs Kuta was pressing against were shaking. As he slept wrapped in his mother's arms that night, he knew it wouldn't be long now. And when the time had come, Kuta's mother had tried to encourage him.

"Kuta, you can never return to the world of women. Today will be a difficult day for you. But I have watched you closely. You aren't a stupid donkey. You are smart. And more than that, you are brave. You will make your father proud of you—eventually. Just be patient." So Kuta had drawn himself to up to his full height and walked out to his father while his mother had looked after him, her face a mask of bitter resignation.

Now as his father turned toward him, Kuta felt like a girl again, but he tried to protect Sunali, who was wide-eyed with fear. And for a reason. Only a few nights before, in the vegetable plot where they listened together, she had looked fearfully at Kuta. She was crying. "Kuta," she had whispered. "I believe what these people are saying." And Kuta had wanted to cry, too, because he knew exactly what that meant. For months they had listened together, hidden behind the corn.

"What am I going to do?" Sunali's voice was much too loud, and after a moment's panic, Kuta's voice was squeaky with tension as he tried to assert his new authority.

"First of all, you are not going to tell anyone. And we are not going to discuss this again." His voice was as hard as he could make it. They had gone back to the house together, curled up on their rattan mats for the night, and Kuta had tried to disguise Sunali's muffled sobs with groans and yawns. He felt numb, and sleep refused to come. But they had still kept listening together, and Kuta had begun to notice a difference in Sunali. She seemed secretly happy—a rare thing among the Muslim women. As she cooked and provided for the men, she was helpful and kind. Even her mother seemed to find less to shout at her about.

Now, as he faced his father, all the courage that had deserted him through the long painful months of his apprenticeship seemed to rush back, and with it a sudden conviction that he believed the radio people as much as Sunali. "We . . . " He stopped, then started again, "I've been listening to the radio, and I believe that Jesus is the Christ, not Muhammad." He was startled to hear his voice so loud and clear, even as he heard Sunali gasp behind him. His brothers and their friends seemed glued to the spot.

His father reached over to Kuta, and his strong brown fingers grasped his thin shoulder. He dragged Kuta inside, into the light, then fixed his son with angry, black eyes. "Say that again, young man, and you'll feel the full force of my rod."

Kuta heard all the menace in his tone and lowered his voice this time: "Allah is cruel, and Muhammad is merciless; but God loves us and wants us to live in forgiveness and joy."

He didn't even see the bamboo rod rise above his father's head. But it flew down with such force on his arm and shoulder that it broke the skin. Sunali fled. His brothers and their friends watched, horrified, then fascinated. Kuta had been whipped before, but not like this. He tried not to cry out, but it was impossible. Blood began streaming from his face, arms, and back as his father laid bare raw flesh, and continued in a frenzy. Screaming, his mother begged her husband to stop, throwing herself in front of Kuta to take some of the blows. Sunali came running back with her grandmother, and the women threw themselves over Kuta as he lay helplessly on the ground in a growing pool of blood. Unless the women intervened in this way, Kuta would be killed.

Panting heavily, Kuta's father threw the rod into a corner and turned on his mother. "Defend him if you want to, old woman, but I refuse to live in a house run by women and children. You can take care of yourselves." And he turned toward the door.

Kuta's brothers were frightened; their father's threat of abandonment was no idle one, and they were not ready to take on the family leadership in this rigidly patrilineal society. Kuta pulled himself up on his elbow and looked at his father. "No! This is your house! What have your sons ever done to you but obey you all their lives? Why should they suffer? I will leave!"

His father looked at Kuta with withering scorn. "For once you're right, you contemptible runt. You will go!" Then he turned to his wife. "You delivered an idiot into the world, now you've turned him into a heathen. He's to be gone by morning. I never want to see him again!" He strode out into the night, and everyone knew he would not return until Kuta had gone.

Her heart leaden, Kuta's mother bound up Kuta's head and bathed his wounds. As he moaned softly on his mat, she prepared some food and a gourd full of water. "Wait a little until your wounds heal, then go to your uncle in Jakarta," she said softly. "He will shelter you."

It seemed a good plan. Northern Sumatra, jungled and volcanic, with its palm oil estates, and rice and rubber plantations, was more than four hundred miles to the west of Jakarta. Jakarta was on the island of Java, the most populous of the far-flung islands of the Indonesian archipelago; his father would have no reason to go there.

Kuta made the journey east slowly, avoiding the jungle, sleeping underneath the rubber plants at night, eating rice, and sweet bananas, and coconut. A week later he was at his uncle's in clamorous, congested Jakarta—Indonesia's capital city of more than four million. But his father had known exactly where Kuta would go, and he was hot on his heels to make sure his uncle threw him out. Knowing he wouldn't be allowed to utter a word in his own defense Kuta slipped out the back door while the two men were talking in the next room. He was now destitute—but, suddenly and unexpectedly, enormously relieved.

Kuta was only one of a swarm of rural laborers hopeful of work in Jakarta at the time. Indonesia's economy was depressed after the slump in rubber exports; the oil boom still ahead. With other indigents he slept in doorways in the poorest parts of the city, waking at daylight, washing his face in the nearest puddle, then making his way to Jakarta's residential sector where he offered himself as an odd-jobs boy to anyone who would hire him.

Often he worked for a piece of bread and some morning tea. It didn't take him long to realize that no one else seemed to be having his good fortune. Kuta began to feel that—as the radio said He would—God was taking care of him. His sense of relief was replaced by gladness, then bounding confidence: God was looking after him. The thought of it put a glow on his face.

Kuta was soon offered regular work on a rubber plantation in Bandung near Jakarta. One of his first purchases was a Bible from Manila, which he sat and read at every opportunity. Watching him one day, a plantation kitchen-hand remarked that the proprietors of the rubber estate read the same book, and it wasn't long before the proprietors themselves came investigating.

"I hear you know more about the Bible than any of our other workers." It was the boss's wife, and Kuta was nervous, but the woman's voice was warm and friendly. She and her husband took a growing interest in Kuta, and from time to time gave him money to visit his parents and family in Northern Sumatra. When he did, Kuta could tell by their stares and puzzlement that they could not believe Kuta's well-being. He found that Sunali, still at home, had bought a Bible too.

As the years passed, one by one his brothers deserted their father's faith for Kuta's, and his father's bitterness toward his sons knew no bounds. When the plantation family at Bandung decided to support Kuta through training at a theological college, Kuta shared what he was learning with his brothers.

He was on his first pastoral assignment when his youngest brother, Manwali, was taken critically ill. Kuta went home urgently, to find his mother moaning softly, rocking back and forth with her arms around her knees. His father was sitting motionless, his face set in anger, and he snarled as Kuta entered: "His great faith isn't able to help him now."

His parents refused to visit Manwali, so Kuta and his brothers went alone to the hospital where the doctors told them Manwali was dying. As they grouped around the bed to pray, they heard their father's voice in the corridor; he had relented. As his parents entered the room, Manwali weakly greeted and thanked them and pleaded with his father to ask God for forgiveness and to believe in Jesus Christ. Their mother, with tears sliding down her cheeks, touched her husband on the arm. He stared briefly at her, then with a long sigh sank to his knees, his hands on the side of the bed. Instantly his wife joined him, and their prayers together were hardly over when Manwali died.

Kuta is a fictional name, but the story is true. The real man lives and pastors today among Indonesian Muslims, where he is said to have exceptional influence. Kuta and Sunali were listening to FEBC out of the Philippines and Saipan.

16
DOUBLE TROUBLE

Manuel had a problem with his conscience: he had a wife and an attractive family of four—and a mistress and two other sons that his wife and family knew nothing about.

He'd had the other woman for eighteen years, almost as long as he'd been married; it was remarkable that no one had ever found out.

Manuel was tall, handsome, enterprising, and successful—a liquid-tongued radio announcer turned wealthy businessman and special franchise holder. He was also head of an influential political lobby group. He lived in Valencia—one of Venezuela's main centers—a city of nearly half a million people.

His bank account was big enough to keep his mistress and their two sons fed, clothed, housed, and educated. If not, they might have made it awkward for him.

He used to think he was obsessed by sex. Any shapely female figure was enough to send his imagination off on a curve of its own. "It seemed my life's object was sex," he said in an account he later wrote. "It was such a deeply ingrained habit that it was like a drug addiction. Even though I hated it, I couldn't stop." He had tried to earlier. As a Roman Catholic, he knew it was wrong, and he'd been a good Catholic: raised on the catechism, first communion at seven, regular attendance at Mass and confession. "But at confession I always repeated the same thing." He went to a couple of spiritual retreats in Holy Week and left determined to stop his adultery, but couldn't. "The retreat was like a shot of anesthetic which works briefly then goes," he writes.

He threw himself into charitable works: taught catechism, joined the Legion of Mary, and did home visitation. But in frustration he finally gave up. "It was impossible for me to beat it. It was bigger than anything I could do." He stopped his regular church-going but kept up his prayers every day, as well as certain charitable acts. "I believed this would add to the positive balance in the final judgment. If I didn't go to Heaven, at least I wouldn't go to Hell." But he couldn't shake off a deep anxiety, and he prayed from time to time, "God, I can't stop this. Take my life if you want to, but please, somehow, save my soul."

He wasn't the only member of his family in difficulties. His daughter, Silvie, a graceful, willowy girl with her father's good looks, had an up and down relationship with her fiancé, César, who had a drinking problem. According to Venezuelan custom the relationship between the two sixteen-year-olds was already considered almost binding, but Silvie was upset about César's drinking. One night when he was drunk she and César had a flaming row, and he left for the park. Simmering down finally, Silvie went to find him but sat down on a park bench to listen when she heard a group of young people singing. As the singing finished, one of the boys came over to talk. "He asked me if I had a Bible and if I read it. I said I didn't, so he started to talk to me about Jesus Christ."

It struck a responsive chord in Silvie. "Somehow I knew this was what I wanted." The boy took her address and told her to listen to Trans World Radio. "He told me how to find it on the dial, and gave me a leaflet about Jesus Christ. I arrived home so excited. I told my mother. I felt something strange inside, and what he had said about Trans World Radio stuck in my mind. That night I found it and listened." She kept listening—for months—usually when she was having her bath or getting ready for bed. The Christ they talked about was alive—"different from the one I knew about. I believed in God, but somehow He wasn't alive."

She was sponging her face in the bathroom one night when the speaker said, "Why don't you accept Jesus as your Savior tonight?" Silvie stopped sponging and stared at herself in the mirror. "I wanted to do this, but I didn't really know how. I was by myself. So I went to the bathroom window and I opened it, and I said, 'Jesus, come into my heart. I accept You as my Savior.'" She wasn't prepared for what happened. "It was as if light rushed in and darkness fled away." She was so happy she laughed and cried. "It was literally as if Christ was born in me. I felt as if a bandage was taken from my eyes." The incident also coincided with the disappearance of some odd things that had been happening since she'd started experimenting with self-hypnosis, yoga, and meditation: once her arms had levitated up from her sides as if by themselves; sometimes she'd been unable to break out of her meditation-induced relaxation; irrational fears would suddenly overwhelm her; and at times her heart would palpitate violently. But—no more.

Silvie concealed her listening from her parents; she knew they wouldn't approve. "But I had to listen. It was as if something inside me was being fed." She began to write to the radio speakers, and they sent her literature. "But I didn't have a Bible, and my parents wouldn't let me go to church or talk to the Christians I met in the park." So after a year she misled her mother and went to a local church instead of a painting exhibition. She felt bad about the lie, and her mother found out anyway.

"She was very angry and even cried," Silvie says. "I told her that this wasn't another religion, just that Jesus Christ had come inside of me now and that nobody could take Him from me. I was almost eighteen. I told her that I was old enough to know what I was doing and to be responsible for myself. She gave me a tongue-lash-ing, so I told her something out of the Bible, and she almost slapped my face." Her father's reaction wasn't as visible, but he was just as angry. But Silvie didn't try to go to an evangelical church again, so the matter was dropped.

Two years later Silvie broke off her engagement to César, and in a small leaflet of several pages that she typed up and gave to her mother for Mother's Day, she explained why. Manuel found the small explanation intensely moving. "It was beautiful," he says. "She said she loved Jesus Christ, but that César laughed at her so much it was impossible for them to be happy to-

gether. But if César changed, then the relationship might be possible. I realized there was nothing bad in what Silvie believed.
As I read what she had written I was moved to tears. I told her
that I didn't mind if she met with her 'brothers and sisters' as she
called them, and I asked her to consider me not just her father
but her friend."

For Father's Day Silvie gave her father a Bible, but Manuel
was annoyed. "I didn't want it. I had been taught the Bible was
beyond the layman, and I just felt she wanted me to belong to
her religion."

But reading matter from Silvie continued to turn up on his
bedside table, and sometimes he would glance at it. He told Silvie she was naive if she thought it was having any effect. But one
pamphlet, "What Is the Bible?" caught his attention, and he
started to read the Bible—"from the viewpoint that it really
might be the words of God." Each night he read a little more. "I
began to feel a change taking place." Then Silvie left a color brochure on the life of Christ at his bedside. Flicking through it,
Manuel came to an artist's depiction of the crucifixion scene.
"Suddenly I felt the presence of Christ. . . . I understood that
He had taken the punishment I deserved for what I had done. It
was something impossible to describe, and I begged God that it
would continue."

Manuel noticed a change in himself as early as the next
morning. "It was marvelous." As he waited at city stop lights on
the way into work, his imagination no longer lingered on the
women who passed. In the following weeks he found he had better control of his language. He was a better boss. "When I was
facing problems, I had a new urge to do what was reasonable and
fair. I was less arrogant."

He said nothing to his family, but Silvie noticed small
changes. "I was very frightened of him; he was a very strong
character," she says, "but he became more approachable, and we
started to talk together more. Later he told me he had had a very
beautiful experience that was impossible to describe. He said he
had felt the Lord and that it filled him from the top of his head to
the soles of his feet."

On a fishing trip, his older brother and some friends asked him what was going on. "We were just saying you're a different person," his brother said. "What's up?"

"Just reading the Bible," Manuel said, slightly embarrassed.

"I wanted to say more but felt I couldn't," Manuel says, "because my adultery—my greatest problem—still enslaved me. I was convinced that only Christ could help me, and I was terribly upset and confused. I finally prayed like this, 'God, I know that you love me and don't want me to do this, so why can't I stop it?'"

Then he had a vivid dream that Jesus Christ spoke to him and told him to separate from the woman if he wanted to go to heaven. Manuel told her the dream, and she recounted one she had just had. "I saw the way into heaven," she said, "and inside were all the saved. But I was not allowed to enter, and I was desperate."

"I shook all over," says Manuel. "I told her what had happened to me and asked her to help me save both our souls, and help me do what I could not. From then on I began to pray, 'Jesus Christ, I cannot free myself from my slavery to this. I'm a prisoner. I can't, You can. You are powerful. Help me.' I begged God insistently in my daily prayers, 'Do it for me.'"

His breakthrough came after a trip to see Trans World Radio's installations on the Caribbean island of Bonaire. Silvie had been begging him for months to fly her to Bonaire so she could meet some of the Spanish broadcasters. Manuel had a private pilot's license and his own six-seater, and he was also curious about the station. As he grasped the international scope of the operation, he was staggered and suddenly felt part of a gigantic brotherhood of believers. It made him more determined than ever to end his unfaithfulness. The following day he listened to a sermon from one of the station's Spanish broadcasters, and the final words rang in his ears: there is great joy among the angels in heaven when one sinner repents.

Immediately when he returned from Bonaire, he took his typewriter to the hangar and hammered out a letter to the woman, telling her everything that had happened from the time he began to read the Bible, pleading with her to believe in Jesus Christ, saying the relationship was over, but promising to continue financial support. In the afternoon he left the letter in her room.

It was the turning point. "From that moment on my life changed completely," Manuel says. "The house and everything in it became more and more foreign to me and literally day by day the attraction I had to this woman lessened, until it was completely gone."

But now Manuel had another problem: how does one tell a wife about eighteen years of unfaithfulness?

Enter Carlota!

Carlota is a small, vivacious woman who talks quickly and excitedly. She says it was only when Silvie broke off her engagement to César that she realized how much her daughter's religion meant to her. When she offered Silvie an expenses-paid holiday to help her get over it, Silvie only asked that she be allowed to go to church. "That said something to me," Carlota says. "It showed me how serious she was about this thing. She really believed it."

When her father finally let Silvie go to church, Carlota went with her a few times, "mainly out of curiosity." After Manuel's trip to Bonaire, she noticed a big change in him, though he said nothing until he began going to the same church as Silvie. Carlota decided to go with them to a church camp, and she turned hot and cold as the speaker finished. "They extended an invitation to people to accept Jesus Christ, and I wanted to put up my hand, but it was glued to my side," she says. "I said, 'God, do something. You raise my hand, because I can't, and raise it high, because I'm small.' So I raised my hand, and that same day I gave my life to Jesus Christ—but I didn't feel any different."

Then six weeks later, Manuel dropped his bombshell. He called the family together and told them everything. But halfway through he broke down and could hardly finish.

Carlota was stunned, then furious. She ordered him out of the house, but Manuel refused to go. Carlota was in full emotional revolt. For nights she was unable to sleep, and finally in desperation she asked God to help her. She fell asleep but woke early next morning and went to the bathroom to be alone.

Suddenly she was struck by the image of Christ, scourged and spat upon, but innocent. "I thought, *If Christ was able to forgive, and He was innocent, then why can't I forgive Manuel?* It was then I realized that I had never forgiven anybody," Carlota says. "I was good to those who were good to me, but if they hurt me, then I paid them back. I started to cry, and I cried for an hour." Then she went back to the bedroom.

"She said she wanted to talk to me," Manuel says. "The look on her face was so completely different. Then she said the most beautiful words I have ever heard her say: 'Manuel, I forgive you. Not only you but her as well. I want you to take me to her house so I can tell her I forgive her.' I could hardly believe it," Manuel says. "I was absolutely jubilant."

"The first thing he did," says Carlota, "was to telephone Manuel Suarez, the Spanish radio broadcaster on Bonaire, to tell him what had happened."

A week later the two families met in Manuel's office, and soon there were other get-togethers. "I forgave the woman, and we get along well," says Carlota. "Her boys also became Christians, and my youngest as well."

Carlota and the unmarried members of her family still live in their spacious, elegant home in Valencia. Silvie married César, on his word that he would follow Jesus Christ, but his commitment soon fell apart and the marriage broke up after some years. Silvie has since remarried.

Manuel only lived another five years: he died suddenly in 1983 of cirrhosis of the liver, brought on by an attack of amoebic dysentery. When he arrived in heaven he would no doubt have expected to look in vain for the incriminating blot in the eternal Book of Records.

17
A WORRYING TALE

Laila runs her fingers through her long, blond hair and pushes her books away. She's three years into her medical degree; the workload is heavy, and the midsummer night is oppressively hot. She pushes her chair back and wanders out onto the balcony of her father's plush home in the affluent Cairo suburb of Heliopolis. It's 11:00 P.M. She looks out at the lights of the city, sighs, then flicks the switch on her radio and tries to find a bit of music. She usually looks for something relaxing at the end of a night's study.

End of year examinations are upon her, and Laila is a chronic worrier. Not that she has any cause to worry: her grades are always high, even though she's two years younger than most other students in her classes. "Hello? What . . . ?" She stops dialing. "Jesus Christ . . . ?" She's stunned for a moment. This is a Muslim country. How . . . ? She fine-tunes the station and listens. Someone called Al Stewart, asking people whether they feel lonely even in crowds? Matter of fact, she does, often. When the presenter signs off, he tells listeners to tune in tomorrow to Monte Carlo.

Laila does. It's a good opportunity to improve her English, too. After a while she writes to Al Stewart, and he sends her something to read. She keeps writing and listening. She learns that one of the Arab radio speakers lives in Cairo, so she makes contact and drops by to talk further about it all. But it sounds too simple. "It's got to be harder than that," she says. The man answers with a shrug—"What can you do to earn a free gift?"

The story is about ten years old now, and Laila is no longer a medical student. She's practicing privately as a pediatrician and general practitioner in a Cairo clinic, an attractive married woman of twenty-eight, a chic dresser, with a ready laugh and relaxed manner, a full-blooded Egyptian in spite of her blond hair and fair skin. She says the programs put her on to something that changed her life. "I should tell you something about myself," she says in excellent English. "I never make rushed decisions. I have to think about a thing one hundred times, and I knew that if I did what the radio said, it was going to make a very great difference in my life."

The word the programs used that bugged her was the word *saved*. "I really didn't know what that meant—except a kind of freedom, and at that moment particularly it meant freedom from my burdens," she says. But what sort of burdens does a seventeen-year-old carry, who is very bright, comes from a stable, happy home, has caring parents, plenty of friends, a very promising future, and a very wealthy father?

Laila laughs, settles back in the chair, and begins to count them on the fingers of her left hand. "Well—there was a lot of insecurity, which was strange because my parents drowned me with love, and not the possessive kind, but the healthy kind. Yet sometimes I felt very unloved. It was a very big hollow inside— though all the people that mattered did love me, and I had everything material that could give me security.

"Then I was lonely. This was also strange because I had very true friends, and a lot of friends. But I felt very lonely inside, as if I was standing in the world all alone—even when I had a lot of people around me.

"And I was frightened of the future. I used to worry about it a lot: what was going to become of me. I would lie awake for two or three hours—just worrying . . . about what might happen, what had happened, even about what hadn't happened! I was afraid of everything in the future and anything that I couldn't see. If I had a small problem, I would worry it into a mountain. For instance, I was so worried about the examination for medical school that I lost thirty pounds: I couldn't eat, I couldn't sleep. And it was so silly because I always got very good grades.

"Also—and this seems so silly now—my parents are very, very conservative, and this frustrated me. If there was going to be a party at someone's house, my parents would always have to know whose home it was, who the parents were, and who was going. At the time I felt grown up, and I wanted to be allowed to act that way.

"And the final thing: I really felt I had to earn this salvation. I had to *do* something to be 'saved.' It's very difficult for a human being to accept something he hasn't worked for; your ego doesn't accept it. I felt this salvation came from doing things and helping people."

About six months after she first heard Al Stewart, Laila decided to try an experiment. It was a night when she felt particularly troubled. "I had all these burdens, and I kept thinking about the things I'd heard on the radio—about Christ being the only way to freedom and happiness, the only one who can save you, and things like that. I'd just heard a program—I don't remember what it was about, but I know it made me realize that God really loved me and that He could take this load from me. So I knelt down, and I prayed and said, 'Lord, I'm absolutely miserable, and they said on the radio that You are the only one who can do something, so I'm going to try this now. Please take my life, the way it is—it's very bad, and it's all wrong; there are a lot of things. You said, "Come to me all you who are heavy-laden and I will give you rest"—and I am very tired. I'm getting a big burden on my back, and I can't carry it any more. So I'm giving You the burden, I'm giving You myself, I'm giving You everything. Please come in now.'

"Well, I wasn't really expecting anything to happen," Laila says, "and I was so surprised when it did. I felt just like Christian in *Pilgrim's Progress*. . . . He's carrying a very big burden, but when he looks at the cross the burden just rolls down the hill. That's exactly what I felt, so light and free, as if a burden had rolled off my back. And I felt so peaceful."

Several days later Laila suddenly realized she didn't feel so lonely. "The big hollow part inside was full. I even started staying at home instead of going out, because I wanted to be with Christ and get to know Him more. I wanted to tell everyone what had happened." She started with her sister, who'd been making her own observations that week. "I thought you hadn't been worrying as much," she remarked.

"It was true; I really did stop worrying," Laila says. "I really felt I had given my problems to someone who would take care of them, so I didn't *have* to worry. This was a huge change, because I had been such a chronic worrier. The things that would have kept me awake at nights, I just gave them to the Lord, and slept." Her sister, who had been listening to the broadcasts with her, decided to follow suit, and their mother knew something had happened to her two daughters because the bickering stopped—not just for a few days but for months.

Then, three or four days after she had knelt to pray, Laila says the "big breakthrough" came. "I suddenly realized that God saw me as perfect even though I was such a sinner, that now I was as white as snow to God. Somehow you still have this picture of yourself as a sinner, and this was what kept me running away for so long: the idea that I had to keep myself white, and I knew I couldn't. Now I *knew* I didn't have to."

It was the grudges that stayed round the longest. "I was the type who could never forget a wrong. If someone did something bad to me I would never forget. It was one of the things that used to keep me awake at nights; lying there thinking how to get even." She laughs. "That one took about three years to go. But I was reading the Bible, I was learning about Christ, and when you start to know Him more, you become more like Him. So at the start it was hard to change, but then it starts to come naturally."

Laila's mother was a practicing Roman Catholic. "She was like me," Laila says. "Because you go to church you think you know everything you need to. She knew Christianity, but she didn't know Christ." Laila used to go with her mother to church because it was the proper thing to do. "Anyway, my mother started asking what was going on, and I told her," Laila says, "but she didn't want to listen for a while. Then one day four years ago we went together to hear a speaker from a church in the Philippines, and for some reason that made the difference."

Laila's father is a highly paid government servant, officially registered as a Christian. "But he never used to go to church or read the Bible or anything," Laila says. "Then my mother started speaking to him, and he started to read the Bible. That's two years ago, and we've seen a big change in him. But there's something missing, and he knows it."

But just a couple of weeks ago, as her father said farewell to a Christian he had spent an evening with, he had remarked to no one in particular, "That man's got something I want."

"What's that?" Laila had asked.

"Inner peace," her father said. *That's interesting,* Laila thought. *That's exactly what I was wanting. It shouldn't be long now.*

18
IXMIQUILPAN

How does one man found 120 churches?

Easy! Just give him a radio.

Ixmiquilpan doesn't even appear on many maps of Mexico, though a calculated guess puts it at between 3,000 and 7,000 feet. Nor do travelers' guides pay the town more than passing mention, and then mainly for its wool weavings, pottery, and silver jewelry.

But Ixmiquilpan also rates mention as an important Otomi Indian center. The Otomi were flourishing in the region well before Cortés and before the Aztecs, and they have steadfastly resisted integration, retaining their own language and culture.

Spanish colonial influence was also felt in Ixmiquilpan because tourist guides also mention interesting colonial buildings and record it as a religious site.

In Ixmiquilpan, religion was first of all Indian spiritism and magic. When the Spanish arrived what they had in mind was conquest: expanding the monarch's realm, finding riches, and Christianizing the heathen. The Spanish church was rich and powerful; cathedrals and churches sprang up. But many Indians just overlaid their ancient superstitions with European rituals and absorbed the saints and the Virgin into their hierarchies of spirits. Other Mexican guardians of the mother faith became fiercely protective of it and violently antagonistic toward any other contender.

Today Ixmiquilpan is a poor, rough, desert town about one hundred miles north of Mexico city, surrounded by mountains. Some farming is carried on, as well as cattle ranching.

Fifty years ago Venancio lived in Ixmiquilpan, a foreman of a farm belonging to a rich landowner. Somewhere he found a Bible and began reading it, and when a construction worker on the Pan American highway challenged him to follow Jesus Christ, he did. The men he worked with began to follow suit and were soon meeting at Venancio's poor house to pray and study the Bible.

The opposition began very soon, but only really organized itself in earnest after Venancio protested that local religious leaders were selling international relief at a profit to poverty-stricken locals. The aid was thereafter routed through Venancio and his growing band, who distributed it free, but Venancio was now a marked man. Angry mobs began to break up his meetings. One member of his group was killed by hanging, another died after he was dragged for a mile through cactus country behind galloping horses. A third was pinned to a church door and his head battered in with a rock when he refused to recant. One villager later told Venancio that, during one murderous foray, the mob he was part of was turned back at Venancio's door by soldiers dressed in gleaming white.

But in spite of the opposition, Venancio's church grew, and as it did Venancio turned his attention to the villages around him, where opposition was just as violent. Twice he fasted and prayed for three days and nights on the tops of the surrounding mountains as he tried to work out a strategy to enter them. His problem was that his co-workers were completely untrained. Then he found a way: someone gave him sixteen short wave radio sets pre-tuned to FEBC's programs out of San Francisco to Latin America. First, he gave one radio to each to his men and told them to listen and learn and spiritually fortify themselves. When more radios came, Venancio began sending them out with his workers into the neighboring villages with instructions to get people listening and left it to their ingenuity.

In the mountain village of Villa Hermosa, one worker, Mercial, tied a rope around his radio, turned it up full-volume, and hoisted it up a pole in the town square; no reactions recorded. Everywhere he went, he took it with him, sitting down with groups of people and turning it on. Out of it came eight churches, which Mercial now pastors, and four preaching points.

Another worker, Precencio, loaned his radio all around several neighboring villages. Out of it came a church in the village of San Miguel de Jigui, which Precencio now pastors. Another, Crecencio, planted his radio in the town square during its noisy religious fiestas and gathered audiences. Radios went with workers all round Ixmiquilpan to a distance of sixty miles, and then out into the surrounding provinces.

Novelty was on Venancio's side when he first began his radio evangelism; there weren't many radios around. But no one— not even Venancio—could have foreseen what the years would bring: 120 churches in four provinces of Central Mexico, most of them with their own church building. Naturally, the largest is in Ixmiquilpan: Venancio's church seats five thousand.

19
RESTITUTION

He was an unscrupulous businessman, capitalizing on the acute shortage of accommodations in Cairo, and when he finally skipped the country, he had about $250,000 in stolen cash on him. He admits it himself: "I robbed about seventy people, and they live miserably now because of me."

He doesn't say exactly how he extorted the money, but it's almost certain that in the two or three years his block of apartments was going up, he sold each apartment three or four times to different clients, taking sizable hard-earned down payments from them all. First occupier in, first served; the other unfortunates lost their deposits and their accommodations. By the time the authorities discovered the fraud, he had hot-footed it to Europe, well out of the reach of extradition treaties.

But he says there was a sort of rough justice in what happened next. He wound up in Italy and, for reasons unknown, was arrested on a completely unrelated charge and given a six-year prison sentence. He maintains he was unjustly accused and sentenced, but he's not too angry about it. "Now I am tasting the misery of my poor victims," he says. "God is faithful and just."

He first writes to Trans World Radio, Monte Carlo, in October 1986, saying he's in prison in Pavia, in Italy's extreme northwest, and that he came across the station's Arabic broadcasts in his cell one night. He has listened ever since on a borrowed radio. "I'm badly in need of spiritual food," he says. "Can you help me find my way to God through Christ?"

He had been a faithful Muslim for years—until about five years ago: "I just lost respect for Islam. I saw how it encouraged killing in the name of God and made it easy for men to get rid of their wives if they weren't pleased with them and marry younger, more beautiful women. I lost my faith altogether—but then I had nothing, and I was no better than an animal." He had never heard about Jesus Christ before—at least not the way the programs described Him. "I was so ignorant when I was satisfied with the little I heard about Christ in my own religion," he says in a second letter. "I was so wrong when I thought that Christianity turned God into a man and that Christians worshiped more than one God. Instead, it shows God's great humility: He left his glory to come to earth to show us how much He loved us. This gives man significance in the universe. This is a God I can believe in."

He asks for an Arabic Bible, and when it comes he spends a lot of time reading it. "The more I read the Bible and the words and parables of Jesus, the more I trust it," he writes. "I really feel that I am one of the sick Jesus came to heal. Certainly I am one of the lost sheep. I wish you had been here when I read the verse, 'Come to me all you who are tired from carrying heavy loads and I will give you rest.' I am certainly tired, and my burden is heavy. Then I read, 'If we confess our sins to God . . . He will forgive us our sins and purify us from all wrong-doing.' How do I confess? Day and night I am asking God to come to me and show me the *truth* and to solve my deep problems. Only God who has come in the flesh is able to do that. I am longing for it."

He asks if he might be allowed to call the broadcasters his family—"though I am not worthy of that, because you are brought up to forgive and to love even your enemies, and I can not do that yet—although I do have peace in my soul through reading the Bible." Then he talks about the fraud he committed in Cairo. "I was one of the people about whom Jesus Christ said, 'What shall it profit a man if he gains the whole world and loses his own soul?' May God forgive me."

His next letter comes four weeks later. "I have decided to submit my soul to the Lord Jesus Christ," he says. "I trust He will accept me. He knows I was struggling at the bottom of a pit. I don't need any more books to convince me now, I want books to help me live as a Christian. I am crying from the depths of my heart, 'Why, Lord, did You leave me lost all these years?' I long to learn how to pray so that I may pray day and night that I and all my people might be guided into the Way of the Lord and be crowned with love and peace."

Hassan has served three of his six years at Pavia, and he's been thinking a lot about the seventy people he defrauded in Cairo. "No one can help my poor victims except me," he says. "I must return to them what I stole from them." And it's clear from his letter that what he has in mind is selling his assets to repay the people he defrauded and facing the lawsuits back in Cairo.

20
A SMALL TRUE DRAMA

Setting: Czechoslovakia
Characters: Father, a communist party official
             Son, a student
             Psychiatrist

Scene One:
  A living room in a middle-class Czechoslovakian home

FATHER *(angrily gesturing toward the radio)*
  How long have you been listening to this religious trash?

SON *(nervously)*
  Well—I suppose weeks now. I found it when I was looking
for some music. It was interesting. I hadn't heard it before. It was
different, and I could believe it. I mean . . .

FATHER *(voice rising)*
  Imbecile! How do you think this looks? Here I am, a member of the communist party regional committee, and you, a son
of mine believing this . . . this insipid, ridiculous philosophy for
fools and weaklings! What do you think it's going to do to your
career? Do I have to watch you throw your life away because of
some idiot idea of yours that you're going to follow Jesus Christ?
If you keep on this way, I'm going to have to pull you out of
school before they kick you out. Pull yourself together before I
have to knock some sense into you!

SON *(defensively, coloring red)*
Well, what I heard was real. . . . I mean . . . I found I could believe it. I meant what I said before—if it bars me from the university, I'll find something else to do.

FATHER *(exploding)*
Fool! Just like your mother! Do you think I've spent all my life knocking the same silly ideas out of her just to have them crop up in you? Obstinate little hound! *(He walks out, slamming the door. Son stays in the room, face fiery.)*

Alarmed that his son is showing symptoms of mental illness, the father decides to take his son for psychiatric examination—nowhere local because rumors might get around. He thinks the capital city might be the best place. . . .

Scene Two:
A psychiatrist's consulting rooms in Prague after two days of observation and tests. The father is sitting on a couch in the waiting room as the psychiatrist appears and invites him into her rooms. He takes a chair before her desk. His son is seated in another like it.

PSYCHIATRIST
Well, Mr. ____, I don't think you need to worry about your son. He shows up as a well-balanced boy, intelligent, and with an outlook more mature than most of his age.

FATHER *(silent, then uncertain)*
But . . . er . . .

PSYCHIATRIST *(soothingly)*
You're obviously worried about his religious attitudes, but I wouldn't let that disturb you. He seems to be the better for it, and you can thank your lucky stars he's not wandering around the streets looking for trouble as many youth are. I'd keep him in school if I were you. I think you'll find there won't be too many problems. He's a sensible boy.

FATHER *(puzzled)*
But . . . er . . . I, er . . . You mean, he's—*(taps his head)* all right? Eer . . .

PSYCHIATRIST
As I said, I don't find anything wrong with him. Our tests show he's well above average. Rest assured. It's clear to me that your son has a sense of purpose that a lot of young people today lack.

Father rises, still looking confused but unable to argue with her professional opinion. She shows him the door. As the boy follows him out, she gives him a warm smile.

PSYCHIATRIST *(whispers)*
You'll be all right! And don't forget, there are many others like us.

SON
Yes. Thank you, thank you very much.

As he walks down the corridor behind his father, he thinks happily of the Bible lying deep in the bottom of his bag. At last he can read for himself the Book they've been talking about on the radio. His father doesn't know it, but the psychiatrist is a believer, a practicing Roman Catholic. She had not only professionally tested him but affirmed him in his faith and made sure that he left with a Bible of his own.

Part 3

I am listening to your broadcasts with some of my schoolfriends. Perhaps our religion hasn't answered our needs because our souls are crying out as if they've been forgotten.

TWR
Turkey

I work in Libya and listen to your Bible lessons in Turkish. I'm curious about God.

TWR
Libya

I am a salesman who spends many days a month on the road. . . . I was not a Christian when I began listening to you, but I enjoyed the non-commercial nature of the station. As I listened to the informative and interesting programs you offer, I felt God's Spirit moving within me. Late in 1988, I accepted Christ as my Savior and have joined a local church. I am planning to marry a Christian woman this year. My life has been changed so since I was saved, I wanted to thank you for the crucial part you played in my salvation.

KMBI
Washington State

I am a university student. I feel ignorant and helpless, but I think what you are saying on the radio will bring great changes in me.

TWR
Turkey

Last August I had a bloodclot removed from my brain. After my surgery, I listened to your station day and night, as there were many nights I did not sleep too well. I can't think of any better way to spend time following surgery.

WDLM
Illinois

It was Wednesday, March 10, 1982, and Mark Lowell commented on a prediction that the world was to end. "Yes," he said, "suppose Christ did make an appearance and take out His followers? What then?"

It was the emphasis on *Suppose He did come that night. Are you prepared?* This really got me thinking, and not being a Christian, I got frightened.

But—I got on my knees and the Lord took it from there. Thank God . . . I just thank God for that night.

So I've been listening for almost a year now, and through it a beautiful change has come about in my life.

TWR
Caribbean

I thank God for WMBV! It has added so much to my life. I was so hungry for the music and preaching of the Word of God your station has provided.

WMBV
Alabama

One night I turned on the radio, and I heard someone speaking about Christ. The next day I listened to all the programs and haven't stopped since. Once you did a series on Psalms, and I had never felt so comforted. Now I read the Bible, and I've come to know Christ. He is always near me, and He has done miracles in my life.

TWR
Kuwait

21

PARIAH

José leans over in his hammock, lifts the long-bladed knife off the crude table, and softly plucks its sharp edge with the thumb of his left hand.

His wife of six years and their four children lie sleeping in a mean shack less than 150 feet away, and José is going to slit their throats: first theirs, then his.

As he stares into the pitch blackness through the long, matted, black hair covering his face, his nails long as a jaguar's claws, despair is a black abyss in his heart. His loneliness is awful, but there are others like him, hiding in the same jungle—disfigured, rejected, refusing all help—fishing from the rivers and lakes and living off the forest: the bananas, cashews, and mangoes. Like him—in about ten years they will die.

It's about 1:00 A.M., and he's only minutes away from the deed—screwing up his courage, perfecting his plan. If he is quick and silent no one will wake; no one will even know. Then he will kill himself.

The low, tinny jangle of his pocket radio on the table merges into the odd sounds of the tropical night, but as he stares into the blackness, the jangle stops and his brooding concentration is disturbed. The local station has closed down. Without shifting his gaze he takes the small radio that has helped pass the execrable hours and turns the tuner, searching for something else—anything. But there's nothing, not here in the watery impenetrable heart of the Amazon jungle. He's about to pick up his knife and leave his hut when faintly, in Spanish, he hears the

words "Cristo es la Unica Esperanza"—"Christ is the only hope."
Hope? If he needs anything, he needs hope! He picks up the set
again, tunes the signal in as clearly as he can, and listens—staring into the blackness. The long-bladed knife is on the table just
an arm's length away.

The program ends, and José stares on into the night, his
mind working over what he has just heard. Spanish is not his
language—he speaks the Portuguese of his native Brazil—but he
has understood enough. Christ? Hope?

José was from Brazil's poor northeast—the state of Ceará.
His mother was a Roman Catholic; his father wasn't anything.
José rejected religion from the outset and grew up a rough,
aggressive man, drinking, dancing, fighting, womanizing, and
spitting contempt at anyone who read the Bible.

In his teens he found his livelihood on one of the numerous
riverboats plying the Amazon and its thousands of miles of tribu-
taries. One day, more than three thousand miles up the world's
largest river, he stopped at Parintins and liked the primitive
town. He settled there, found work on the local boats, married
in 1965, and had four sons.

He lived in his explosive way until 1971, when he found he
had leprosy. Like many others, he had no idea where or how he'd
caught the dreaded disease, but it was the sentence of death, and
with the odd logic of the Amazon leper he fled into the jungle to
hide, refusing all medical help until he died. But his wife and
family didn't desert him; they lived close by and brought him
food.

But anger, loneliness, and then murder filled his heart. For
months now he had wanted to go on a violent rampage, killing
anyone he saw. Tonight he had focused his lonely desperation on
himself and his family. . . .

. . . Hope? Christ? He looks down at the small radio, his
murderous resolve momentarily forgotten. He doesn't touch the
tuner—he might never find the signal again if he does. He wants
to hear the early morning broadcast the presenter announced as

he signed off, so he lies the rest of the night in his hammock with the radio on, waiting.

When the program comes on the air hours later—"Manancial da Vida, Fountain of Life"—faint as the signal is on the tiny set, José hears it through. It's a long shot, but at the end he decides to try the new Way the radio was talking about. That was fourteen years ago.

That night at the end of 1971, José's life underwent a transformation that got the rough town of Parintins talking. The wild recluse is now one of the city's identities. Today, locals in the rough city of sixty thousand when giving directions to each other, often say ". . . near the house of José the Leper."

José is still a leper today. Although medicine has slowed the spread of the disease, it hasn't cured him—it was too advanced by the time José finally let anyone treat him, almost three years after he heard the life-changing radio program.

He lies now in his woven hammock in his tiny, blue, two-room, weatherboard hut, talking and playing with a dirty piece of muslin rag. He's about sixty-five, but his hair is still black, and he's still a good-looking man in spite of his leprosy. A ginger kitten squirms ecstatically on its back under a table covered with a blue plastic cloth. Odd memorabilia and clutter spread along a simple wall-shelf: the first Bible he ever owned, a photograph of the staff at Trans World Radio on Bonaire, a flower, a calendar, several pictures, and a small TV set.

A powerful Panasonic receiver has replaced the small pocket radio. His hammock is strung diagonally across the room, his crutches lie against the wall, a noisy fan slaps at the humid air. His wheelchair is in the next room with a few utensils, a bunch of bananas, and a large pan in which his wife, Lucimar, bathes him every day in warm water liberally dosed with penicillin. She has to fetch and carry the water; there's no local water supply.

It's the same spot of jungle in which he hid years before, but Parintins has grown so much that he now lives on the city's ramshackle urban fringe. The risks of infection are still too great for him to live with his family, but they are just across the road, and the kids—there are five now, teenage and older—come regularly to see him. They're all on daily doses of leprosy preventive, but even so, no doubt because of her closer contact with him, Luci-mar also has leprosy. But the better medical facilities and drugs, and the speed with which her symptoms were discovered, mean that she will be cured.

The change that got everyone talking began the night he first heard the programs, José says. As he speaks, one eye rolls up into his head, the other out to the right, a side effect of the drug he's on—Sulfone.

It was the second program that hit him hardest, he says. "They said Jesus was the Truth, the only way, and the true life, and I'd never heard this before." But it was John 3:16 that really broke him open: God loved the world so much that He gave His only son so that everyone who believes in Him will not die but have eternal life. He still repeats it to himself whenever he feels lonely or depressed.

Since that night in 1971 José has never missed a program. Slowly, he taught himself to read by matching the words he memorized from the radio with the meaningless shapes of print in the Bible in front of him. Not really welcomed at church because of his leprosy, he learned most of what he now knows from the programs, and his memory, sharpened by years of illiteracy, turned him into a walking Bible lexicon. He steadily earned a name as a counselor and teacher-extraordinaire; people would come in droves—up to one hundred each month, individually or in small groups—to sit at the doorstep of his hut and listen to him dispense counsel from the fund of stories he had heard and scores of Bible verses he had memorized.

Just out of interest—who was his last visitor? José pauses a moment. "Last Friday a man came who was very embarrassed and desperate," he says. "He'd heard the radio, and he came to get the Trans World Radio broadcast schedule so he could tune in." José reeled him off the schedule, which he keeps in his head. "The man came again the following day," says José. "He said he'd enjoyed the programs very much and didn't want to miss any more."

Five or six years ago José was still able to get around the city, and locals got used to his amiable but hardly delicate ap-proach: "Are you a Christian? Do you want to accept Christ?"

But now, because of the spread of the disease, he is unable to get around except on crutches or in his wheelchair. Doctors amputated his left foot several years ago, and the lower leg is now wrapped in a bulbous bandage and covered with a black sock; José keeps it out of sight as best he can. In his dangling and twisted right foot, the disease is still active and the pain can only be controlled by drugs. His right hand is badly deformed—the classic "claw" of leprous neuritis—his left hand less so. For medication he takes sulfone drugs, iron tablets, and milk; a month on each to balance the intake. Apart from his leprosy, he is a healthy man with a healthy appetite.

On Saturdays, Lucimar helps him into his wheelchair, and he sits in the doorway of his hut looking out over the property—which he has imaginatively modeled after the Garden of Eden—and he preaches to those who come. He turned his 4,500 square feet of jungle into an Eden because he reckons heaven is going to be a garden like the one God gave the first human beings on the planet. It's now a sort of miniature tropical park, decked out with seats, special lighting, mango, orange, and cashew trees, and brilliant, tropical flowering shrubs.

José may die of old age before he dies of leprosy. He says he will die if Trans World Radio ever goes off the air. "I know all the announcers by their voices—they are like a family to me. I feel I live with them," he says. He still never goes to church. "But I have a church inside my house."

A tropical downpour rattles on the hut's corrugated iron roof and rushes onto the ground. It's impossible to talk. It's the start of the wet season, and the Amazon will rise more than thirty feet. In the bog that Parintins becomes in the wet season, he will be completely house-bound.

But José will stay in his hut, reading, listening to the radio, and talking to visitors. He's not afraid of anything, his friends say. In an area where 12-foot snakes are not uncommon, he sleeps with his door wide open.

His eyes roll up into his head, and he tucks his amputated foot out of sight behind his good leg. He says he's looking forward to getting up to his Garden in the Sky. "This I know," he says. "I am a man of a lost body, but I have a saved soul."

22
FEET AND MILES

How far is 350 miles? Not far by plane. Much farther by car, farther still by bus, and a long, long way by foot, horseback, and canoe. Longer still when you are very poor, crippled in your feet, and traveling through the equatorial rain and heat of rural Colombia.

The doctor at Hospital Vozandes-Quito looked at the two women, astounded. "You wanted to come to this hospital? All that way, just to this hospital!"

Rosa could only nod. To her it was all very simple, as she explained. Up till about a year ago, the family earned a good living growing coca for the cocaine barons. That is, until a man had told them about HCJB, and the family had listened and decided to become Christians. But they could not be Christians and continue growing coca, so they pulled up their coca plants and planted rice. Their income plummeted; they barely made a subsistence living, but at least they could live with their consciences. They couldn't get to church; the nearest church was hours away, so church became a daily family event around the radio, where they also heard about HCJB's medical arm, Hospital Vozandes in Quito.

So when an operation on eighteen-year-old Doris's feet became imperative, it was irrelevant that it could have been performed easily at almost any clinic. Hospital Vozandes-Quito was clearly the place to go. They had no money, but God would help them.

The operation on Doris's feet was successful, and Hospital Vozandes bore most of the cost of the surgery. As Doris recovered, she and Rosa plied the hospital chaplains with questions, and this time, as they hit the road back to central Colombia, the miles flew by.

23
VILLAGE BIBLE SCHOOL

China: a vast and backward country, teeming with the largest population on earth—more than 1 billion people—most of whom are peasants. In fact, eight Chinese in every ten are peasants. Put another way, one person in every five living on the earth today is a Chinese peasant.

For centuries the Chinese peasantry has been an exploited class, but at the turn of the century most peasants lived in grinding poverty. Extortionate rents, taxes, and interest payments to landlords and moneylenders had reduced them to destitution. If their land wasn't seized in payment of debt, they were taken as slaves. They were starving and illiterate. Their work was backbreaking, their technology primitive. At the mercy of fighting Chinese warlords, they were often drafted at whim into private armies.

It is not surprising, therefore, that they were stirred into the gigantic peasant army that swept Mao Zedong and the People's Republic of China into power in 1949 on promises of relief and reform. And there were reforms: land confiscated from the elite was divided out to the peasants, and agricultural production shot up. With the end of the civil war industrial output rose by half. The fifties were promising years.

But Mao's Great Leap Forward—the attempt to transform China into a developed economy overnight—was a spectacular failure, and it coincided fatefully with several years of bad floods, drought and famine, and the withdrawal of Soviet aid. The return of hardship brought the pragmatists: leaders who encouraged material incentives and bonuses, new technology, small private plots, free markets, and men who set about building an enormous bureaucracy to implement it. All too much for Mao, the ideologue, to whom the changes reeked of "revisionism," a slavish imitation of the imperialist capitalist systems to which a xenophobic China had closed its doors in 1949.

So began the Cultural Revolution of 1966: a vicious assault on anything associated with pre-Revolution China, capitalism, and foreign cultures. Nothing survived that was not subjugated to the party. Mao's ruthless Red Guards went on a rampage. Educational institutions were closed, intellectuals dismissed, publication of literary and scientific journals stopped, library collections destroyed, and all books banned that did not promulgate the sayings of Chairman Mao. Temples were ransacked, monasteries disbanded, churches destroyed, believers persecuted and killed. And on the peasant communes, where 80 percent of China lived, loudspeakers everywhere boomed out a relentless party propaganda and the new culture: a tiny and sterile collection of dramas, operas, and songs that glorified Chairman Mao and the party ideology. The Chinese *People's Daily* has published a figure of 100 million who "suffered" over the ten years of the Cultural Revolution—the true figure is no doubt higher.

But the Cultural Revolution had one outcome Mao could never have anticipated. It brought about the mass production of transistor radios with short wave and medium wave bands to propagate the party line. Though few peasants wanted to hear the propaganda, a radio was still a novelty item. But they were priced beyond the peasant's pocket, so the Politburo made radios dirt-cheap, and a luxury item came within the reach of China's poor. Peasants in droves bought them and found they could pick up religious broadcasts in Chinese from outside China. The word began to get around.

FEBC Radio began broadcasts into China in 1949, just after the Communists came to power. There was little response. No one dared respond; the risks were too great. To the Communists any religion was a superstition, the opiate of the masses, a tool of the ruling classes. But Christianity in particular was the religion of the foreign intruders of the last several centuries and a symbol of wealth and privilege. The Red Guards were brutal in eradicating it.

At the time the vast majority of Chinese practiced ancient superstition, spirit worship, and magic, combined with any one or all of China's three main religions: Buddhism, Taoism, and Confucianism. Christians were estimated at less than 1 million. Since 1949 not much has changed in the attitude of China's rulers to religion, except for a state-managed easing of the ban on religion in the early eighties. But the number of Christians is now widely held to be more than 50 million. Some communities are known to be entirely Christian, some 50 percent, some 10 percent. The church has had her martyrs in China, and their blood has been its seed, but that alone cannot account for such a staggering growth. Radio is held to be mostly responsible. Since 1949 the number of FEBC programs into China has grown to almost forty hours a day—from Saipan, South Korea, and Manila —in five major Chinese languages: Mandarin, Cantonese, Swatow, Hakka, and Amoy.

But the burgeoning Chinese church had a problem. Its leaders were ill-equipped to teach their mushrooming congregations. When a flood of letters swept out of China in the late seventies as China opened its doors to the West, FEBC set about analyzing a sample of thirty-five thousand letters to identify church leaders and their special needs. It became clear that they desperately needed training. No leader in the sample had had any theological training; many had become leaders not because they knew anything about the Bible but simply because they possessed one or because they had copied out radio sermons and passed them around. A third had been Christians for only two years.

FEBC's response was Village Bible School, a program specially designed to train church leaders in China's peasant villages. It went to air in 1985 and now runs four hours and thirty minutes each day, a combined effort of nine production centers and forty staff. Basically it is theological training by radio. Village Bible School offers forty-eight subjects over three years, each lasting thirty-nine programs. The material is constantly being reviewed and improved and has been recently expanded to include radio back-up cassettes and course-summary textbooks, which are distributed inside China. Each textbook is about fifty thousand words, and eighty thousand copies are printed of each. Most reach their destinations. Of the extensive range of subjects offered, the most in demand so far have proved to be Daniel and Revelation, basic Christianity, the life of Christ and church history.

Response to the programs has surged from 6 percent of the total Chinese mail response to 20 percent in four years. It is clear that the broadcast meets a need in the peasant village communities as letters tell:

"Dear Teacher: We have formed a church. At the beginning there were only 10 of us. Now we have 300. But I am still ignorant of the Bible. I can only learn it from your programs. They help me so much. Please pray that your books arrive safely" (December 1988).

"A few days ago I received the Village Bible School notes. I jumped for joy. I become so immersed in them that I forget to eat. I accepted Jesus by listening to your program. After a year, when I felt I was able to explain the Bible, I began holding meetings in a place near my home. Now our church is the most prosperous in the district and has been registered. Can you send me a reference Bible?" (May 1988).

"The books you sent me last year were confiscated in a persecution by the United Front Work Department. Then they tried to stop our worship, but I argued that it was legal because it was indigenous. We finally won. I rely on your broadcast to shepherd the church here. I listen to you morning and night. I take my radio to the fields. Everyone says that no one here can explain the Bible as well as you do" (July 1988).

"This year our church has grown tremendously; literally day by day. Young people come early to pray and study the Bible. They often discuss Village Bible School. They listen every night. I am baffled by the questions they ask. We are in great need of your notes on the New Testament, Pastoral studies, Daniel and Revelation, and the Four Gospels" (September 1988).

"As I was praying I was so overwhelmed by our lack of materials that I burst into tears and could not sleep. We are starved spiritually. Please send us your Village Bible School notes. They will help me understand the Bible and share it with my brothers and sisters" (December 1988).

"We are a group of university graduates. Many of us listen to your broadcasts. Village Bible School is particularly helpful to us. But we have difficulty revising the lessons. Can you send us your material?" (January 1989).

"I am an engineer and a translator. My friends are intellectuals. They are all eager to listen to the Gospel. I am thinking of starting a house church to help them know God. Please send me all your Village Bible School notes" (February 1989).

"Your lessons are a tremendous inspiration to me. We have organized ourselves into a Bible Study class here, and we really want your notes. We listen to your programs every day" (October 1988).

"The authorities are always pressuring us. They won't let us hold Bible studies or prayer meetings. But we are managing to hold one evening Bible Study Class, and people from neighboring villages come. Most of us are illiterate. Please send the notes on Daniel and Revelation" (undated).

"We have been listening to your broadcasts for two years now, particularly because your Bible exposition is so good. You have taught us a lot. We sing, pray, and share God's Word for an hour and a quarter every evening. There are about 20 believers in our village" (undated).

No doubt the numbers of letters arriving at FEBC offices in response to Village Bible School will keep climbing as long as it continues to meet the concern expressed in one letter from the southeast of China. "The number of believers in my village has doubled and tripled," the listener writes. "The churches are crowded. But it is very difficult for anyone to attend a theological seminary. Who will take care of all these people?"

Through Village Bible School, FEBC is answering: "We will do all we can."

24
"THIEF"

Never lock a teenage kleptomaniac in his room—or he might find a radio and develop a "psychiatric problem."
This was certainly what Ji Sheng's parents thought he had after he'd been listening for a while to some of TWR's Chinese language broadcasts. They weren't sure which was worse—to have a son who was a compulsive thief or one who listened to religious broadcasts.

Ji Sheng certainly had a name for himself in the neighborhood: if anything was ever missing, people always came to the Ling's place to find it. Sure enough, that's where it would be, secreted away in Ji Sheng's room or somewhere around the house.

It had got so bad they had to lock him in his room each night to protect the neighborhood. He did most of his petty thieving at night—so no more evenings out with friends. Eventually his friends stopped coming. Ji Sheng spent most of his time locked in his room, doing his homework and playing with the dial on his shortwave radio. So it wasn't surprising that he came across the broadcasts from Guam to the Chinese mainland.

He found the programs interesting—or so he said one day when he decided to write to the broadcasters in Hong Kong. "I've learned a lot from you that I didn't know before," he said. "That there is a true God who created man and the world. I have also learned to pray, and I've learned your songs. I've found out what is in the Bible, and I'm telling others about it, too." Actually, the kids at school were already calling Ji Sheng a "Bible nut" because everything Ji Sheng heard on the radio at night he told them at school the following day.

But nuts or not, he found one thing had changed for the better: he could control the impulse to steal.

"But good times don't last," he said in his letter. "When my parents heard me talking about God and Jesus all day, they thought I had a psychiatric problem. And when they found out about the radio, that was the last straw. They moved it out of my room and wouldn't let me listen at all—even though I had stopped stealing completely and no one came to our house complaining anymore. I thank God and Trans World Radio for bringing the message of the Bible to me."

The radio remained out of bounds for a year, and if his parents ever found him listening they gave him a thrashing and made him go without meals. "But I didn't forget God, I just kept Him in my heart. When I was able to, I prayed," Ji Sheng said. "But I badly wanted to listen to the radio, and I was always arguing with my parents about it."

But on the third day of the new lunar year his mother lifted the ban for one program, "The Good Earth," and this time listened with him. She was pleasantly surprised. "You told us how to schedule study time," Ji Sheng wrote, "and I'm so grateful because my mother said to me, 'This station isn't so bad after all, much better than it used to be. I can understand why you like it.'

"When I heard her say that, I gave her a hug and said, 'Mom, can I become a Christian?' and she said, 'Yes, as long as it doesn't affect your studies,' and I was so happy that I burst into tears. Thank you for the program that day."

Ji Sheng reaches the end of his letter: "There are very few Christians here, and it's very hard to study anything about Christianity," he says. "But I really want to study the Bible. Do you think you could send me one? Oh, and don't forget to send me a program schedule, will you?"

25
CRY IN THE NIGHT

Mary is too frightened to use her real name, so she's chosen an alias—a "Christian" name. She lives somewhere in North Africa, in one of the larger cities. Or, at least she did then, but she may have left the country by now. Though given the circumstances, that's unlikely.

Her letter comes with no return address—a deliberate safeguard; if any return mail were opened by her family, life would be miserable.

Mary is obviously intelligent, not only because she has studied French, English, computer programming, telex, typing, science, and law at the university level, but because she managed to get into the university at all. (Not many students do, and most who do are male.)

She's now twenty-eight years old and has become personally convinced that she should be a follower of Jesus Christ—a conviction that now puts her outside the protection of the law, because in her country no one of the majority faith may convert to Christianity. But, in the final analysis, the state may be gentler than her own relatives, who might privately and summarily decide to enforce the letter of the law themselves.

Even as she writes, Mary faces probable disinheritance by her family—maybe even a vengeance killing, and certainly social discrimination in a thousand-and-one different ways.

She writes that she tuned into a Trans World Radio broadcast in the Arabic language late one night and found the words strange at first. "But as I kept listening, I began to love Jesus Christ." After a period of time she doesn't specify, she decided to make the break with her inherited faith but wanted her change of heart to be visible. The only course she knew was to be baptized—a step someone like Mary only takes when she is prepared to die in consequence.

Mary also writes about another pressing problem: marriage. Her family is putting heavy pressure on her to marry, for she is more than ready: pretty, educated, and well into marriageable age. She wants to marry a Christian, but that would be a scandal—not only that but it would be illegal. "But I have decided to follow Jesus Christ," she says. "How can I marry a man who is not a Christian?" She feels that if she marries and keeps her faith secret, she would fail Jesus Christ, who has won her heart. If she marries, then "owns up," her husband might cruelly snuff out her faith. If she refuses to marry at all, the shame she would bring upon her family, and the opprobrium upon herself, would be almost more than she could bear. She could leave her family and country for an independent life overseas and the freedom to marry a Christian, but in this part of the world young girls are reared to be dependent on their families.

She writes in Arabic pouring out her heart:

"My childhood was not a happy one. My father was cruel to my mother. I used to love my mother very much and hated my father for the way he treated my mother. But my father loved me and tried to win me over to his side to make my mother jealous, though I never let him, and he began to hate me. None of this did me any good, of course, and I used to lose my temper a lot, not only with my father but also with others.

"Life really started for me at school. I don't know why, but I developed quite a reputation for myself. I wasn't at the top of my class, but I was clever, sharp-witted, and ambitious, and I wasn't afraid of my teachers, even the tough ones. I also used to like befriending Christians, and again I don't really know why. Most of my friends were Christian girls, and occasionally I used to wear their crosses on my big golden chain. I just liked doing it.

"At the end of my first year at high school I had a dream, which I remember now as clearly as if it happened last night. I saw Jesus standing in the air. He was beckoning to me with both hands while I was standing with my friends on the campus. I stretched out my hands to Him joyfully. Then the dream ended. I was afraid to tell anyone about it in case it got back to my father. Anyway, as the years passed I forgot about it. I went on with my study, sat my college entrance examinations, and passed with honors. My father died that same year.

"I enrolled at the Faculty of Science, but at the end of the first year I got sick and failed my exams. I transferred to the Faculty of Law, but again, at the end of the year, I got sick. I didn't give up, though. I studied English, French, computer, telex, and typing—and passed everything. But I felt empty all the time and didn't know why.

"Then about two and a half years ago I started to question a whole lot of things in my religion. Why this, why that? My brothers and mother told me to stop it and got angry with me. But I wasn't afraid. I kept asking questions and learned my first truth, that my religion was a lie—no more, no less. But in a way it was worse knowing that, because then I had nothing—no religion.

"At this time I met a guy who said he was a Christian, but it was clear from the way he talked that he was an atheist, and I was very confused. It only became clear what he really believed when his brother changed his religion just so he could marry the girl he wanted. It was obvious he had no convictions at all, so I broke off my relationship with him, and I was crying on my bed one night when I turned on the radio. And there you were. At first I found the words and ideas strange, but I kept listening every night at 11:30, and finally I wrote to the programs and even gave my address, but I never heard anything back. So I just became completely fed up, and that made me feel even more hopeless.

"Then I remembered the dream I had in my first year at college, and somehow I began to love the Christian faith. This was the second truth I discovered—that the Christian faith was true. I used to wait for those evening programs all day. The days went by, and often I asked Jesus to get me out of the mess I was in. I was very upset because I didn't know how to become a Christian or how to find anyone who would listen to me, let alone help me. Then I met a Christian girl, and I told her everything. She arranged a meeting with a priest. I saw him twice, but after that he refused to meet me again. He taught me a lot and gave me some cassette tapes to listen to, but he refused to baptize me. I told him I was ready to leave my family and everything I had and to emigrate, and he said, 'Well, in that case you can get baptized outside the country, because I'm scared that if I baptize you people will hear, and I will be in trouble.' It was enough that he taught me, he said. This really upset me because I wanted to be baptized. I lost confidence in everyone, but I continued to read my Bible at night."

Then Mary came to her most pressing problem: What does a girl do who has repudiated the religion of her family but is under enormous pressure to marry the man of their choice?

Most young girls in Mary's shoes bow to the family's wishes, because marriage in these cases is not an affair of romantic attachment and choice by two young lovers, it is the family's choice, particularly the father's—a marriage inside the father's extended family if possible, and if not, then a match with a family of equal social standing, to strengthen the economic and political standing of each. It is awkward and excruciatingly embarrassing for a family if a daughter continues to reject such suitable arrangements and outrageous if she does it because she has become a Christian.

So she will hope to influence her new husband. She may succeed, and she may not. She will rarely have the courage to start a new life in a strange land so she can marry the man she wants to. If she refuses to marry, it will be a wretched existence . . . putting up with her family's continual contempt and rejection while she continues to live with them. For in her culture, it would be unimaginable if she left home.

Mary is struggling with all this as she writes: "I am twenty-eight now, and many young men want to marry me because I am pretty. My youngest sister and all my relatives have got married, and I am the only one left. Everybody is trying to marry me off, and I can't keep on saying no forever. If I keep on much longer, there will be rumors of immorality.

"At the moment a perfectly eligible man wants to marry me, and I can't keep telling my family I'm not interested. I went to a priest, and he told me, 'Marry him, what else can you do?' This upset me, and I said to him, 'How can I marry him? He is not a Christian, it is impossible! I am a true Christian.' But he said to me, 'What else can I say to you?' and he abandoned me.

"I believe and am sure that Jesus will not leave me. I love Him and have crowned Him King of my life. I surrendered myself to Him, and I know He will not leave me. He has changed me completely. I am a lot more patient, long-suffering, and courageous. He has given me tranquillity and wisdom in place of anxiety and depression, and many people have noticed the change. These are beautiful qualities Jesus has given to me—especially patience.

"But in the name of the Lord Jesus I beg you to help me. I am begging the Lord Jesus for mercy, and He knows how I am suffering and struggling. I know you will hear my cry. . . . I cannot mention my name in case your letter to me is opened in the mail. But I will call myself Mary and place myself in God's hands and yours."

Mary

Of course, no answer could be sent. It can only be assumed that Mary kept listening to the radio. No broadcaster will ever know how she fares today—unless she writes again.

26
AQUEDUCT

In the town of Segovia in the old Spanish state of Castile, birthplace of the nation of Spain, one of the world's best-preserved Roman aqueducts still stands, its giant arches vaulting the basin that cradles the busy town center.

The farming village of Maella is about forty miles from Segovia, too small to appear on most maps—a slightly derelict, parochial place. The white plaster overlay on the small mud-brick houses is cracking and falling off, shops behind anonymous exteriors do a desultory trade with a few customers, a few old denizens unaccustomed to strangers stop and stare, squinting in the harshness of the sun. Here and there a few new houses look conspicuous in their fresh, white plaster.

In the winter it can be viciously cold around Maella, but in the summer the place is an inferno. In June the air is dry and still and heavy with the heat, and nature itself seems scarcely able to breathe. By midday temperatures have already reached 40°C (104°F), and the sun is a burning orb in a merciless sky. It's madness to stay outside, so the people of Maella withdraw behind their green shutters into the coolness of their simple, whitewashed interiors and wait for the scorching sun to dip toward the west.

In all of Spain the heat has a way of displacing the afternoon's activities into the evening; the Spaniard goes very late to bed and rises equally late in the morning. And it's obvious, when you see Domingo Triviño at 10:30 A.M., that he hasn't been up long. His blue eyes are red-rimmed and encrusted with sleep, and he hasn't shaved yet. You take a second look and change your mind—hasn't shaved for days.

Domingo is sixty-seven. The thongs on his leather sandals are broken around his dirty feet. An old blue beret is jammed firmly onto his gray close-shaven head, and a dirty brown cardigan hangs over his blue corduroys. It's only when he walks that you realize why he leans, when he stands, on a rough-hewn stick with a knobbed handle; his small frame is almost spastic with the effort of walking. A closer look and you see his legs seem deformed; so are the fingers of his left hand. Later, he tells you he's been a cripple since birth.

Life has kept Domingo so poor that the limits of the province essentially constitute the boundaries of his world. A monthly trip to the church at Segovia is about the only traveling he does. But he's sharp, and his reading and radio listening have made him a mine of obscure bits of information.

He takes you down to the village park and children's play area—a small, overgrown, roughly fenced plot—and you pick your way to a log table shaded from an already ferocious morning sun by a few trees.

Domingo's voice is a growl, and his speech comes in rapid bursts of strong, almost unintelligible Patois. His toothlessness doesn't help his enunciation; one prominent bottom eyetooth seems all that's left. But he's an enthusiastic individual and overjoyed to talk.

He was born in the village and has never left it. His father, a farmer, died of pneumonia when he was only one year old, so Domingo and his mother moved in with her parents while she worked as domestic help around Maella to support herself and her only son. Domingo's grandfather was a man subject to sudden, violent rages: he almost knifed the priest the day Domingo's mother was baptized. The priest was new, she was his first baptism, and it was meant to be free of charge. But the priest was going to make them pay, and grandfather was so enraged he pulled a knife on the priest, and a fight broke out in the church. About a year later he suddenly drowned himself in the water tank on the hill. No one knew quite why, except that he'd got into a fight, come off second best, and it had become a paranoia of some kind.

So his mother was forced to Madrid to find work, and Domingo stayed with his grandmother until she suddenly became a paralytic, and he was deposited with an uncle. His uncles spent all their time fighting, he remembers, then cackles. "One of them had a filthy temper, and the other had a screw loose." Life was lonely; but he had one close friend whom he called Manolo.

At the public school on the plaza he learned to read and write better than most of the kids in the village, and family funds were good enough to keep him at school until he was fourteen, when he started work as a farm laborer. His crippled legs limited him to simple work, but he toiled long days with hand-plow and oxen, renting himself out to the same two or three farmers each season; turning over the fallow ground, plowing in the fertilizer, then furrowing for planting. The day started at 6:00 A.M., broke for a midday siesta, then continued till 9:00 P.M. when the sun went down.

He was in the village plaza one day getting sacks to pack straw in when some girls—foreigners—handed him a bit of paper. Curious, he took one home to read but couldn't make any sense of it—something about God, salvation, works, and grace. But it mentioned the Bible, and Domingo had been thinking of getting a Bible so he could read it for himself. So he wrote away to the address on the pamphlet to enroll for a course of Bible study. When the course arrived, there was a brochure inside giving some radio frequencies and broadcast times of religious programs in the Spanish language. So he began tuning them in regularly.

Domingo adjusts his stick, blinks hard, and takes off again in his rapid, staccato Patois. "The reception was poor, but I listened very carefully because I wanted to know what was in the Bible. The programs were very important to me." It was a long time ago, but he remembers something about the Tower of Babel. The builders of the tower were planning a rebellion to unseat God. Men were like that; and he implied—as he was obviously meant to—that he was also like that. He remembers a series on the life of Jesus Christ. As he listened he did the course, and he had to answer the question, "Do you consider yourself to be a 'son' of God or a 'creature' of God?" He wrote down creature, because that's what he thought he was. "I believed in God," Domingo says, "but I was frightened of Him. I knew He was holy and that I wasn't."

When the instructors of the correspondence course wrote back, they suggested he stop being a creature and become a son of God, and they enclosed a pamphlet describing how. This time he understood what he read: God had emptied His anger against man onto Jesus Christ, who had suffered instead of Domingo. There was nothing else Domingo could do to be accepted by God than to believe it. So he had believed it. "I felt different immediately," he says. "It was a sense of relief, I *knew* my sin was gone." He signed the card they sent him, saying he had accepted that Christ was the only way to peace with God, and they wrote back telling him there was a church at Segovia where he could meet other believers.

His mother didn't like what he'd done. The stout, blue-eyed, white-haired old lady was seventy-nine then, ninety-one now. "If I read the Bible she got upset," Domingo says. "When my friends came from the church at Segovia, she would always tell them I wasn't home. She fought me every inch of the way." But in it all he experienced, *really* experienced, an imperturbability and strength of purpose that he knew weren't his own. "Especially strength of purpose," he emphasizes. For the following twelve years he continued to care for his difficult old mother, and Jesus Christ had become a personal help, encouragement, and comfort he could always rely on.

Everyone in the village soon learned what had happened to the crippled Domingo. He went straight to the mayor of the village for permission to use the civic hall to show a film about Jesus Christ—which was granted—and he began to talk openly around the place about what had happened to him. The villagers found it all a bit eccentric—but Domingo was a good man and one of them.

Domingo gets restless. He's concerned about his mother, who's still in bed. "She'll be needing me now," he says. "She can't get up without me." Domingo and his mother rent the ground floor of one of Maella's better buildings—at modest rates by special arrangement. Domingo can afford it because his disability pension is bringing in a whole lot more than he ever earned as a farm laborer.

Has Domingo ever been bitter at God for the way life has treated him? It's obvious the question surprises him. There has been real hardship and poverty. But for Domingo it doesn't matter. Not in the least.

27
I LAID MY BURDEN DOWN

"I figured I was no different from anyone else," Nihalyne says, tucking some stray strands of white hair back under her black head scarf. "At least if I went to hell there would be plenty of others there like me. I wouldn't be there by myself."

Nihalyne is a widow in the small, rural village of Bér in northcentral Hungary. "I believed in some vague way that God existed," she says, "but there was no evidence as far as I was concerned. "I couldn't see Him or talk to Him. I was always saying, 'Show me the proof.'"

About five hundred people live in Bér, and the road Nihalyne has in common with her neighbors is just a wide, uneven expanse of dirt—at the moment the property of a dozen geese. They scatter, squawking and flapping, as you approach. Her garden is bright with flowers. A young dog scampers up to investigate as you walk up the garden path, and clucking hens scratch at the earth by the back door. An ivy, tinged with autumn, clambers along the wall of the house and over the gutterings, and on the window sills seeds are drying for pounding and cooking.

Nihalyne appears. She's been slaving over the stove, preparing sweetmeats and a late lunch for her son and his family, and her face is the color of the ripe apples on the window sills. She's dressed in black, the traditional garb of the Hungarian elderly and widowed, and she greets you barefoot, apologizing she's been caught so unprepared. Inside the place is clean, open, and sunny, and begonias are flowering on large window sills.

Nihalyne was born in Bér. She's about sixty-five now, and the house you've walked around is the one her husband built himself—before he died. She's delighted to see you and insists on feeding you generously. Sweetmeats over, she takes you into the lounge—the drapes are drawn, and the darkened room is obviously little used. She sits down at the table and waits for the questions while you take comfortable chairs.

Her husband was only forty-one when he died. It had been a happy marriage, though materially things hadn't been easy. He had just built the house, and their son was only weeks old when he was sent to fight at the Russian front in 1941. He caught a bad blast of shrapnel in the head. Epileptic seizures started, which got worse after the war. Back home he worked hard on a collective farm, and hard work always made the epilepsy worse. "I used to plead with him, 'Don't work so hard,'" Nihalyne says. "But he said he had no choice."

Ten years after the war, she came home one day and found him hanging in the attic. She was thirty-eight. He'd left a letter, but it didn't help. "On the first page he explained—or tried to explain—why he had committed suicide," Nihalyne says, "but the second page was just a complete jumble. I went through an awful time over it." She doesn't explain. "But now I give thanks to the Lord God. I laid down my heavy burden." But not immediately. For twenty years she carried on, blaming herself somehow for his death—knowing the neighbors were talking—raising her young son alone, working hard to keep enough food on the table.

Gall-bladder problems started and pain began in her feet. Her son got married, and she felt unwanted, deeply weary, and alone. "I longed for someone to love me," she says, "for some sort of comfort and release from it all." It was then that several people told her about religious radio programs in Hungarian from Monte Carlo. But she was skeptical because she'd never been a church-goer, and she'd always done her best to stop others going. If she was anything, she was Lutheran, and stoutly of the opinion that if people insisted on going to church, then they should go to a Lutheran church: something that was Hungarian and not some foreign import—like the Baptists. But she listened to the pro-grams, and over several years her interest became a hankering.

"I found I really wanted the kind of life they were talking about, and anyway I was at the end of my tether," she says. The broadcaster kept telling listeners to find a church if they wanted to become believers, so finally Nihalyne went to a church—a foreign import! "The first sermon I heard was Jesus' parable of the workers in God's vineyard," she says. "Some workers began working in the morning, and some late in the day, like me, but they all got the same wage. So I realized it didn't matter that I'd come to God late in the day and that I wasn't young."

Then she heard another Bible verse: Jesus saying, "Come to me all you that labor and are heavily laden and I will give you rest." It was all she needed to hear. Something happened, and she let her load go. "I laid my burden down," she says. "That's my story. I put down a heavy burden."

That was in 1978, and she was fifty-eight. She kept going to church and listening to the programs. She hefts a big, power-ful, shortwave radio receiver onto the table. "This is what I lis-ten on." Her bright blue eyes flicker up. "You must never stop the programs. They give us strength for each day and answer our questions." Her grandson appears, and together they pose for a photograph. He often listens with her.

Her sense of relief was so great after she laid her burden down that she talked about it everywhere—and still does. "I can't put a lock on my mouth. Every evening I talk to someone about Jesus Christ." Having let go her own burden, she's become concerned about everyone else's, and many people carry plenty, she says. In conversations with villagers, she finds they're sick or anxious about something or just plain idle. She tells them they should listen to the programs and read the Bible—tells them what happened to her. When she leaves her neighbors, they usu-ally find the family radio tuned to Monte Carlo.

She's a tonic to have around . . . doesn't believe in hold-ing grudges. "Some people hold grudges, but you mustn't take these things to heart; you only hurt yourself," she says. Maybe it's because she is no longer "hurting" herself that she says she no longer needs her medicines.

The cornflower blue eyes light up, and she smiles. Has she always been a smiler? "Yes, I've always been a smiler," she replies, "but these days it comes from the inside."

Fred and Aliw Magbanua
The Philippines

FEBC

28
ORDINATION AT 308 FEET

It really takes something to swing from a piece of metal by your
hair—especially when your hair isn't very long, and you're 308
feet up a tower.
You could expect a few things to be flashing through your
mind: "Is this really happening to me?" or "Exactly what *is* happening to me?" or "This has to be it! Curtains!"
But what flashed through Fred's mind wasn't any of those
things. It was his own voice, recorded on tape earlier in the day,
and he heard it loud and clear. He was reading a couple of lines
from the Bible: "My brothers, I appeal to you: offer yourselves as
a living sacrifice to God, dedicated to his service, and pleasing to
him."
Fred didn't hang by his hair for very long, only a few seconds—just long enough to hear his own words resonating inside
his head and long enough for ten to twenty amps of high voltage
electric current to burn most of the hair off his head and scorch a
hole into his crown. At that moment Fred became a human radio antenna. Ten thousand watts of electricity-bearing, highly-
amplified radio waves vibrating 702,000 times a second jumped
from the hexagonal mat at the top of the transmission tower onto
Fred's head, just at the point when they were about to leap from
the mast and hurtle horizontally at the speed of light out into the
Philippines. That portion of what was destined for the Ilonggo
speakers of the Philippines that day ricocheted around the inside
of Fred's head instead, and Fred will say God intended it that

way, because he needed to hear his own message more than anyone living in Ilonggo land.

An electric shock of ten to twenty amps is a nasty one—
about equal to a vicious bolt from a couple of domestic electric
ovens. It was enough to knock Fred unconscious, and it could
also have stopped his heart. It didn't, but it administered some
nasty third-degree burns.

What do you do when you're 308 steps up a transmitting
tower and you're knocked unconscious? Well, you fall, usually.
And from that height, probably to your death, slashing yourself
on the way down on the sharp steel trusses bracing the tower.
That didn't happen to Fred. When the electric current released
him he was already unconscious, but as he began to fall his leg
jammed in the ladder. That, and a worker's platform only four
rungs below, arrested his fall. When he came to some minutes
later he was lying in a heap on the platform, his knee locked
around the ladder, and his head aching excruciatingly. On the
ground no one knew what had happened; he was almost out of
sight, lost in a mesh of steel bars.

Fred had been about to quit for the day when he noticed
that the big mandatory red bulb on the top of the tower had
blown. Broadcasting regulations required the mast to be lit by
sundown at one hundred foot intervals. The compound work-
men had retired for the night, and it was just dusk as Fred threw
the switch that grounded the tower, making it safe to ascend. No
one really knows what went wrong: engineers guess at humidity
corrosion in the switch, or perhaps faulty electronics. Maybe
someone turned it on again; Fred's own weekly, fifteen-minute
program, "Tingog Sang Kaluwasan," produced that morning in
the studio, was about to go on the air.

Whatever happened, the tower was live as Fred climbed it.
And Fred had completely forgotten about his program. He was
within a foot of the antenna when the pulsating electric current,
always seeking a path back to earth, chose his head as the most
convenient point to start the return journey.

It was a Sunday, and when Aliw, Fred's wife, saw him coming down, she asked the domestic to lay the table. But Fred never
had supper that night. He just barely made it the one hundred

fifty yards to the nurse's quarters on the thirty-acre FEBC compound, then collapsed unconscious. The Manila Sanatorium admitted him as an emergency patient, and X-rays showed a dark spot on the brain—a sure indicator of very serious brain damage. But although Fred remained in the hospital for skin grafts and brain scans for three months, the specialists never found brain damage. Fred was heartily relieved, but in a way he wasn't surprised.

The problem with Fred was that he had a sort of wanderlust. He was twenty-nine, sharp, well-educated, warm-hearted, and a qualified civil engineer—he could have gone places in life. But he had meant it six years earlier when he told God that he would devote himself to "the ministry." However, after three years with FEBC as compound engineer and announcer, working hard for a small salary, and with a young wife and two young children to support, he was thinking again. And when a college friend wrote from the United States saying he was recommending Fred for a civil engineering job in his firm at an excellent starting salary, Fred wanted out.

Aliw was dubious when Fred shared the letter with her. "You made a promise, Fred," she said reproachfully. "I know," said Fred, "but think of all the good we could do with that money."

"You made a promise," Aliw repeated.

"C'mon Aliw," Fred coaxed. "We could help support five pastors on that sort of salary. I can't do that on what I get here."

"It sounds like a good idea," Aliw said after a pause. "But there's something wrong with it. You did make a promise."

But Fred's mind was already made up. He would record his program that morning, then write to his friend accepting the offer. He was still thinking about it when he threw the switch to the tower and began to climb.

Recovering in the hospital, Fred had ample time to think things over. He saw again the small Filipino boy of nine obsessed with the fear of death; saw again the Japanese invasion in 1941 and the atrocities and disease that made the prospect of death even more petrifying and personal, especially when it claimed two of his ten brothers and sisters; saw again his religious family, the trips to church with his grandmother as early as 4:00 A.M. Though what he learned about life after death didn't relieve his fear of dying: if his good works outweighed his bad ones, he would go to purgatory, otherwise to hell.

He remembered June 1949. He was seventeen when he heard the FEBC radio program that banished the specter of death; heaven was only as far away as a prayer for forgiveness. It was significant to Fred that the tower that almost electrocuted him was the same one that broadcast the radio program that day long ago. He thought of his vow never to take a secular job, his decision to work for FEBC as compound engineer, the dissatisfaction and all the tempting job opportunities, and all his justifications.

Aliw's rueful words hung in his conscience. "But Fred, you promised!" And he *had* promised. But there he was preaching on the air ". . . offer yourselves as a living sacrifice to God . . ." while he was preparing to leave the country. So God had turned the verse around on him—and almost fulfilled it.

At the end of three months in the hospital and another month for plastic surgery, Fred had settled the matter in his own mind: he would keep his promise.

Fred's renewed promise is twenty-seven years old now, and he has never broken it. He doesn't climb towers anymore though, he climbs organizations. Today, he is the Managing Director of Radio FEBC (Philippines)—the organization he very nearly deserted. He is also a senior board member of numerous Christian organizations and something of a statesman in the Filipino Christian community.

Marks on his crown and head from the burns he received are still visible, but his hair has long since grown back. Fred is fond of referring to a Philippine Roman Catholic custom as he gingerly touches the dent in his crown. The church has a practice of ordaining its priests by anointing their crowns with a slightly acidic emulsion. "Tell Father X that he might have been ordained by his bishop eight feet off the ground," Fred is reported to have once good-humoredly snorted. "But tell him that God Almighty ordained me when I was three hundred feet off the ground and there was no one else in sight!"

29

DRIVER

"What?" Janos muttered to himself. "What for?" And the brows of his cheerful, open face furrowed in an uncharacteristic frown.

The telegram was brief. "Report to Party Secretary, 8 A.M., Tuesday next." No reasons given! Reporting to the secretary could only mean one of two things: you were on the mat for something, or it was party matters.

But Janos wasn't a member of the communist party, and he wasn't sure what he'd done wrong. But he had a sinking feeling it had something to do with his "visibility." "Father Janos—the company priest," the other drivers called him. It was a running gag.

Well, Tuesday was four days away yet. Janos tried to put the matter out of his mind. He'd worry about it on Tuesday.

Tuesday dawned—and as he knotted his brown regulation tie, Janos grimaced. "It could even be the ultimatum. Oh, well, so be it!" He shrugged on the brown jacket, grabbed his green cap—the uniform of the Volan bus driver—and clattered down the outside stairs, glancing at his vineyard as he did. It had been a bumper crop this year, and he'd given a lot of grapes away. Even made a bit of his own brew, too. Wasn't too bad.

As he pulled the double gates shut behind him and looked back at the pleasant, solid, middle-class family home with its big, well-tended garden, he winced at the thought of losing his job. He was forty-seven, and it wouldn't be easy to find another. He

still had a fifteen-year-old son to support, and home maintenance took its share of the budget . . .

"Kiss, Party Secretary wants to see you!" His boss sounded
concerned. Janos gave him a quick nod and a thumbs up, then
checked the bus into the traffic controller for repairs. Trust the
thing to break down on the way in—now he was late, half an
hour late. So the controller knew about it too—the word had obviously got around. "You'd better get off to the Party Secretary,
hadn't you?" he said as Janos dropped out of the big bus. "Don't
report back here till you've seen him."

"You're late," was all the Party Secretary said as Janos entered. "You were meant to be here at 8:00 A.M.."

"Yes, I know. Sorry. Bus troubles," Janos said, and remained standing.

The secretary picked up a sheet of paper on his desk.
"We've had a complaint that you're listening to religious radio
broadcasts on duty," he said evenly, not looking up. "You know
company policy."

It was impossible not to. State companies just reflected the
official religious position: atheism. And Volan Buses wasn't just
a little regional company; it was the national bus service.

He thought rapidly. *Who, when, where . . .? Ah! Just a moment . . . that man at the railway station several weeks ago!* He was
meeting the train and waiting for the mail, and as he sat waiting,
motor idling, a passenger had said to him, "Turn off that radio."
And he'd turned it off.

"What's so bad about religious broadcasts?" Janos asked the
secretary mildly. "You can get religious services on Hungarian
radio."

"Yes, but that's different," the secretary said. "They aren't
imported."

Janos had listened on the bus to the Hungarian-language
broadcasts from Monte Carlo for as long as he could remember:
as long as he had been driving with Volan buses, and that was
thirteen years, and even before then, when he'd been one of
their mechanics. When he started driving, he'd installed his own
shortwave radio in the bus dashboard—all according to the rules.

"We won't sack you—this time," the secretary said, suddenly looking up at him. "But this is a warning. What you're doing is quite unacceptable."

"Won't sack you." Janos felt his whole frame relax in a silent sigh of relief. But then he suppressed a snort. "Unacceptable!" A lot of things were unacceptable on the buses. Bad language was one of them, but he heard it all the time. He almost said something but decided not to.

The secretary was silent, and Janos racked his brains for something to say. He had one of the company's best safety records, but that was no defense. He listened to the broadcasts every day, morning and evening, and the passengers often listened with him. But this was the first time there had ever been a complaint. He said the first thing that came into his head. "Ah, I won't bother that passenger again, sir."

More silence, while his mind was suddenly flooded with recollections. He'd lost count of the number of times passengers had asked him to write out the frequencies and broadcast times; they'd even asked him to turn the volume up so they could hear better. Some even asked if the same program was going to be on today that was on yesterday. He used to let passengers get on the bus early on Sundays so they could listen with him until he pulled out. He'd had his share of deprecating remarks, true, but usually good humor wasn't too far away. "You praying again?" one of his passengers had said just the other day when he'd turned on the radio. Usually he switched on by familiar landmarks en route. He prided himself on his punctuality, and he was so punctual that he was rarely more than a couple of seconds off on a broadcast—even though he drove 240 kilometers a day.

The secretary was speaking again. "You know the rules, Kiss: no problems with news broadcasts, music, and local stations. But no more of this foreign religious stuff. Understood?"

Janos understood very well but thought of the times he'd used the programs to help his passengers when they confided in him: that woman the other day being beaten up by her husband. She'd shown him the bruises. She'd wanted to divorce him, but when she'd asked him what she should do he'd told her a story he'd heard on the radio, and encouraged her to stick with him. "Try to help him. Maybe God will work a miracle." The teen-

ager with lots of boyfriends had told him tearfully that their interest never lasted. So he'd used an illustration to explain to her
what real love was all about—and marriage.

Suddenly the interview was over, "Well, that's it, Kiss,"
the secretary was saying. "I'll file a report saying I've seen you."

He got up from behind his desk, came around to Janos, and
lowered his voice. "Aaah . . . of course, I listen to Trans World
Radio myself now and then. Aaaah . . . off-duty, you understand."

The expression on Janos' face barely changed, but his ad-
am's apple bobbed furiously as he swallowed hard to smother an
overwhelming urge to seize the secretary by the shoulders and
kiss him resoundingly on the cheek. But he said nothing, and the
secretary moved behind him to show him the door. Janos left re-
spectfully and reported for duty.

"Here he is!" One of the drivers raised his voice as he saw
Janos coming. "Here comes the priest!" Janos grinned. The usual
ridicule. "If I'm the priest round here," he shot back, "then why
aren't you guys listening to me?"

He'd seen the secretary a number of times since then, and
the man had made a point of coming over and saying hello. "We
should get together a bit—as believers, I mean," he'd suggested
tentatively the other day.

It was interesting, Janos reflected as he eased the big bus
out of the terminal and started his sixteen-hour shift: it wasn't so
much the authorities that gave you the hard time. It was your
mates! He'd joked to his boss the other day, "I think I'll be a
priest." He didn't really mean it; he was just thinking of taking a
Christian leadership course.

His boss had looked at him sideways and said, "You going
to be a priest or a bus driver?"

Janos had grinned, "I'll stay a bus driver until you throw me
out."

His boss returned the grin, but he was serious as he said, "I
hope you don't go. We don't want you to go."

Janos looked at his watch—10:30 A.M. Oops, the morning's events had almost thrown him off schedule. Almost time
for the next broadcast. As he throttled back and pulled into the
curb for a couple of passengers, he reached over and switched on
his radio.

30
SOMETHING UNWANTED

She was fifteen years old—very selfish, very pretty, and very intelligent—when she found she was pregnant.

She hadn't taken any precautions; she always thought it would never happen to her. Naturally she would abort; an infant was an unwanted intrusion. So she tried everything she knew in the first three months to force a miscarriage: took pills, gave herself injections, lifted heavy objects, and took cold baths at 3:00 A.M. on winter nights. But nothing happened, so at three months she decided to have it aborted. She borrowed money and was about to secretly admit herself to the hospital when she suddenly decided to call a male pen-pal she'd been writing to for two years in a city some distance away.

You can't see Viviana or even hear her voice. She is a young Argentinian somewhere in the city of Buenos Aires. The only voice you can hear is her translator's, on tape, but she is obviously talking freely in her native Spanish.

"I was scared to death about the abortion. I'd never called him before, but I wanted to tell him the whole thing—I don't even know why. I talked for an hour and a half, and I cried all the time." She wasn't prepared for his response. "He was quite calm; he told me about God and God's love, and how important children were, and what they could become. He told me about my mistakes and about the Bible. He told me a lot of things I didn't understand, but they comforted me. He told me to tell my mother and said he would pray that, when I told her, she would be compassionate."

Viviana told her mother next morning. Her mother cried, hugged her, and said that a child was a blessing from God. As the live-in mistress of a married man still living with his wife, she probably figured her daughter's teenage pregnancy was inevitable. Her pen-pal's advice changed Viviana's mind: she decided to have the baby. "That was when I started to dream dreams, and to like the idea of becoming a mother and to feel love for my child," she says. But she had no intention of marrying the father and setting up home. She wanted to rear the child herself, remain single, and study for a career.

The parents of both families tried to get the pair to marry, but Viviana would have none of it. Her mother persuaded the baby's father to move in for several months, but Viviana hated him and at times wanted to kill him. His name was Carlos, he was twenty-three, and he was everything she had ever wanted: handsome, dashing, romantic. They had met in the bright, mad whirl of Carnival—the huge, Argentinian folk-festival that surges through the streets and squares of Buenos Aires before Lent and produces a regular crop of babies nine months later.

It was a miserable pregnancy: she was sick, confused, deeply depressed, and cried a lot. And she was angry. "I was furious at everything that lived. Sometimes I was almost hysterical. I had such a temper that I scared everyone away." At nine months, the baby had to be delivered by Caesarean after a long and unfruitful labor. It was a boy, and Viviana called him Fernando. But she never felt the elation and excitement she expected. "I just felt a complete failure. I thought it was all going to be easy, but the baby had suffered, I had suffered, and Carlos didn't care about anything." When Viviana arrived home he left, and her mother was furious.

Fernando was a colicky baby and cried continuously for six weeks. The doctors were no help. In addition, Viviana felt rejected, despised, and gossiped about. Her mother had a friend who was a medium, so Viviana began going regularly for cures for Fernando and curses on her neighbors. The woman doused her clothes and Fernando's with strong perfumes, but there was no improvement in Fernando's condition, nor did ill-fortune befall her neighbors. She felt like a trapped animal. "I was totally disillusioned. I would escape downtown without Fernando and want to smash myself against a wall." But the courage to take her own life failed her, just as it had many times in the last eighteen months when she had sat with a gun to her head, unable to pull the trigger, or opened a vial of her mother's sleeping pills and tranquilizers and poured them onto the palm of her hand.

After three months she had lost all interest in Fernando. She fed him, but left everything else to her mother and despised advice. She tried to revive her relationship with an early boyfriend and visited the medium more and more often. At home she was arguing with her mother over her responsibilities toward the baby. Viviana's de facto father often escaped next-door to bellyache about Fernando and his mother, and the strain they were on his pocket. The neighbor's wife heard it all and invited Viviana and her mother to a local evangelistic crusade and to ask for prayer for Fernando.

"Well, what do we lose if we go?" Viviana argued with her mother. "It can only be something else that doesn't work." So they went, and Viviana was soon bored. She also felt conspicuous. But she perked up when the speaker came around to his subject—the occult: spiritualism, palmistry, astrology, ESP, reincarnation, astral travel, subjects that had fascinated and occupied Viviana for years. She had studied to be a medium and enjoyed the sense of power it gave her. Her sign of the Zodiac ruled her day, her love affairs, and, just recently, even her pregnancy.

But this was no enthusiastic endorsement she was hearing. Viviana was puzzled: spiritually dangerous, psychologically destructive, he said. Viviana was shaken. She'd never heard this about the occult before. Then the preacher talked about repentance, and forgiveness, and following Jesus Christ. "I related all these things to the way I was living, and to my child, and decided I had to make some response," Viviana says. She glanced at her mother and saw she was standing up in response. Viviana stood too. It marked the beginning of a change: new friends and visitors, regular church attendance. Fernando's health picked up, and someone found her a good pediatrician. There was even a little more peace at home, though it didn't last long: her stepfather didn't like the churchgoing or the visitors.

During her pregnancy Viviana had occasionally heard a radio program—"Revista Radial"—half an hour of interviews, music, and advice around a theme. It was religious, so Viviana had never paid it much attention. Nor had she wanted to hear any advice. But just after the crusade, she heard the program again as she was doing the housework and, when she heard the subject, sat down to listen. It was a two-week series of six programs on child-raising in the first few years, with special focus on the mother-child relationship, the mother's attitude, and especially the child's need for love and touch. Viviana listened to them all.

"Your child will become what you make it. If you neglect him, he will grow to despise you," she heard. The speaker reeled off statistics on the fate of neglected children. "Teach him from the Bible, take him to Sunday school." Viviana was mortified. "I did a lot of crying in those six days," she says, "I could see what an awful mother I had been. On the last day I took my child, and I hugged him and asked God for forgiveness. I cried and cried for all the harm I had caused my baby. I accepted my responsibilities as a mother and discovered the goodness of God in the growth of my baby and in my influence upon him."

That night Viviana wrote to "Revista Radial." "I have been childish and selfish. I have planned everything without taking him into account at all. I've failed completely as a mother. I've left the baby in my mother's hands, as if she was the mother and I wasn't. I want to grow to be a mother. I have a lot to learn, but I am sure that from now on our lives will be different. I've offered my life to God to be a true mother."

And she meant it. "His crying stopped as I accepted him and loved him, cared for him, and paid attention to him," she says. He changed. He began to sleep more, eat better, and be calmer.

She kept listening to "Revista Radial." Traveling with her stepfather in the truck, she would tune the program in, in spite of his impatience. "I *had* to listen, everyday. It helped me so much."

Fernando continued to improve but was still sickly. Specialists in Buenos Aires, five hundred miles to the south, advised her to move out of the tense atmosphere at home. A year ago Viviana moved to Buenos Aires, joined a local church, and now lives and works in a children's home, caring for the children and for Fernando. At times she wants to run away. "But I know it's all part of growing to be somebody," she says. "There's a lot in my character that needs changing, and if I don't let it happen now, then when? They are good people here, and they have welcomed me. Fernando is growing, and really I am very encouraged."

Viviana still plans a career, either as a psychologist, teacher, or nurse. She's seventeen now and plans to study more as Fernando grows. But whatever she finally does, one thing is clear: she is determined that Providence, not Pisces, will make all the important decisions.

Part 4

An Xhosa man born and raised in the Transkei worked in the diamond mines in South Africa to earn enough money to buy a wife. He settled down on a small plot of land and tried to make a living from a few cattle. Children were born. Sometimes they went to church. When drought struck, his small landholding turned to dust. Day after day he and his wife hoed the dust and waited for rain. . . . It never came.

He left again for the mines, and lonely for his wife and children, he bought a radio to shorten the evenings. One evening he heard singing in his own Xhosa language, and a message, "You must be born again." Kneeling by his radio in the mine compound, while others stared at him, he asked Jesus Christ to forgive him and save him. He wrote a letter to his wife and children, "You must listen to these programs," he said. "From them flows the water of life."

TWR
South Africa

I am a Christian by name only. I heard your program about the prodigal son, and I realized it was about me. It opened my eyes to many things, the most important one being that I know very little about the faith I profess.

TWR
Poland

When I turn your radio station on, my thoughts are directed to Christ. That is marvelous! Both the Word of God as it is taught and the music of praise help me to be able to move forward.

WMBI, WMBI-FM
United States

An unknown bus driver in the Indian state of Maharashtra started his long inter-state journey at 4:30 A.M. At 5:00 A.M. when Trans World Radio came on air from Sri Lanka in the Marathi language, the driver pulled over and stopped the bus. "Listen to this," he told his passengers and turned the volume up. His captive audience really had little option. It was half an hour before the bus resumed its journey.

TWR
India

Needing something new to listen to on the radio, I just "found" WDLM and have been listening to it ever since. WDLM has been that counseling I needed! Everyday! I just would not be the same person right now without the counseling of the "Minirth-Meier Clinic." Those people have brought sanity into my life.

WDLM
Illinois

I'm a new human being since I started listening to Trans World Radio. I started listening January month. I used to drink a lot of beers, whisky, etc., to forget my problems, but it became worse. Then I used to go to sleep early, get up early 3 or 4 in the morning, start to do housework, but it were even more worsed. I were a nervous reck, but thank the Lord for Trans World Radio.

I am forty-four, and I learned a lot of things through the Bible by listening to the preachers. I used to play radio whole day, but since I started listening to Trans World Radio I save my batteries for night Trans World Radio program. You all have saved a soul. I have learned a lot through the Bible. I am a new regular listener.

TWR
Venezuela

31
FEAR

"I remember thinking, *Now I'll hear the clock strike two at any minute.* I was crying and crying that the Lord would help me . . . that I wasn't too bad . . . that He would accept me. Eventually I fell asleep, and when I woke up in the morning I couldn't believe how different I felt."

Jean Sadler was forty-six, and she had a personal problem the size of a mountain: she literally went into paroxysms of fear every time she had to go anywhere. She never went outside the boundaries of her father's property if she could help it—not even to the village shops—and she was terrified of enclosed spaces.

As a child she was a sickly little girl who played alone by the hour with small lead animals—taking them to market and buying and selling them. At school in Pottom, England, she was frightened of the boys, and it didn't get any better as she got older, which was why she never married. When she left school the thought of getting a job terrified her, so she stayed home and worked on her father's small-holding.

If the family went anywhere in the car, she was sick with anxiety beforehand. Trips into London were a nightmare, and she always hoped something would happen so they couldn't go. Even the occasional three-week visit to Grandma in Suffolk reduced her to nervous prostration.

One of the worst ordeals she ever had to face was confirmation at the age of twenty-one in the local Anglican church. Her mother had told her that if you went to church, knew the commandments and the creed, everything would be all right. So although the confirmation classes and compulsory attendance at a couple of church services hung over her like the sentence of death, Jean figured that, if she wanted to get to heaven, she would have to go through with it.

To help her, her parents persuaded a next-door neighbor to go with her. Jean went to the shortest services, sat as close as possible to the back of the church, and slipped out during the singing of the hymns. Confirmation over, she retired with great relief behind the four walls of her parents' home and basically stayed there for the next twenty-five years.

If she was forced to sit inside a building, she made sure she had the nearest seat to the door so she could bolt for the exit if she had to. She never used public transportion or escalators. Relatives tried to get her to join them for a day at the seaside but never succeeded; at the age of forty-six she had never seen the sea and never worn a swimsuit. Her parents didn't really know what to do about it; they used to tell her to pull herself together. But it made no difference. It was only when she reached her forties that Jean began to realize that her life was a pathetic waste, but she felt powerless to do anything about it.

She's perched forward now on the edge of a comfortable lounge chair in her parents' house about forty miles north of London, sipping tea. It's midwinter; snowdrifts are lying deep outside. Jean is a small, slight woman with short, dark, straight hair, a ready, toothy smile, and heavy-rimmed, thick-lensed glasses, which enlarge her eyes. But the mousiness has been replaced with a lively impishness, and her face is bright with enthusiasm. She says the change has been enormous since the incident five years ago.

Jean wasn't just forty-six and living like a hermit—she had a spectacular temper that occasionally sent chairs flying. She was also haunted by a fear of death that woke her at nights and made her morbidly anxious. On the conscious level she didn't believe in life after death or in God, so it didn't make sense that she was so frightened. "I thought like Dad, that death was the end," she says, "and yet I couldn't get rid of this idea of an angel with two books: a big one full of all the bad things I'd done and a small one with the good things."

Sometimes she thought that perhaps God did exist—that is, on the occasions she listened with her mother to the BBC Sunday morning religious program. She even thought at those moments that she might become a Christian, but the feeling always went away. One day the announcer said Billy Graham would be talking on the program about death. So she prayed, "If there is a God, please say something to me." But the program was unhelpful. Nevertheless, she decided to take the correspondence course the program advertised, and with the course material came a magazine, *Hour of Decision*, which advertised a radio program of the same name. Thinking it might be broadcast by the American Forces Network, she tried to find it on the radio but couldn't. Instead she ran across Trans World Radio. It wasn't "Hour of Decision" that she heard, but what she did hear made her stop and listen because it had the same style to it as the magazine.

So she began to listen each night at 10:45 and soon found she was regularly hearing talk about people being born again. She also prayed that she would be born again and that her life would change, but the weeks went by and nothing seemed to happen. She came to the conclusion that she was past redemption—too bad to be saved. The end of most programs would find her in tears, vowing never to listen again. But the following night she would switch it on again.

One night she heard a program that seemed to have been written just for her. She can't remember the speaker, but the words are still very clear. "He said our sins were buried deep in the sea and that when God buried something in the sea He put up a 'No Fishing' sign." Then the speaker told a true story of a girl who thought she was too bad to be saved. "Though her reasons were different from mine, I felt God was telling me I wasn't too bad for Him to save," Jean says.

She went to bed that night, praying and crying, and finally fell asleep about 2:00 A.M. "I was crying and crying that the Lord would help me . . . that I wasn't too bad . . . that He would accept me."

As Jean tells the story, the change occurred overnight, while she slept. She went to bed upset, desperate, begging God to save her, and when she woke up she felt as light as air. "I felt as though a great weight had gone. I felt so different." The oppressive fear of dying had simply vanished. "All I knew was that it was going to be wonderful to meet the Lord Jesus and that I had no need to fear," she says. She couldn't stop singing one of the program signature tunes: "Isn't the love of Jesus something wonderful." "I'd heard the tune so many times, and I knew that's what I had to sing. I even beat the eggs in time to it; it was in my mind all the time."

In the days that followed she began to feel her prayers were getting somewhere. The sense of praying to a remote being who might or might not exist was replaced with confidence. "I knew He was there, and I knew He accepted me and was interested in me."

Even the temper tantrums lessened. Not only were there fewer of them, but if she felt one coming, "I would pray quickly, 'Lord, help me.'" No more chairs went flying.

She wanted to go to church, but the fear of people and enclosed spaces returned. "I thought, *How can I? People will look at me and say, What's she coming for after all these years?*" But a neighbor gave her an unexpected invitation to hear the Salvation Army band, and she jumped at the chance. "I said 'Yes,' and Mum was surprised, because she knew how afraid I was of going anywhere. I said, 'Yes, I'm going. It's a Royal Command. The Lord has arranged this. I must go.' Anyway, I wanted to go."

Once she was inside it wasn't so bad. "The people were friendly." She sat in the middle of a pew, people all around her, and felt the old panic rising. But then I thought, "No, I'm a new person, I don't have to worry about that now." Then she largely forgot herself and thoroughly enjoyed the evening. "I got interested; the words all made sense, which they hadn't before. It didn't really bother me what people were thinking. I was enjoying it. I knew the Lord wanted me to be there."

Jean kept going to church and decided to make her faith public one day at the end of a special service. She was shaking all over as she testified to being a Christian. She also told them she wanted to be baptized.

It's five years now since Jean put her head out of her shell and looked around, and she's come a long way out since then. The woman who had never seen the sea bought a swimsuit and startled the family friends by accepting their standard annual invitation to the beach. "They were so surprised to see me getting ready and that I went off so hearty." The frightened, self-conscious woman who would never play the piano if anyone else might hear her now regularly accompanies fifty women in a weekly sing along. The agitated, claustrophobic, bespectacled little woman who would sit near the exit in any closed space so she could run if she had to now enters crowded halls and churches as a matter of course. The woman who hated having to go outside the front gate now travels alone into London without second thoughts. The phobic little stay-at-home who was too terrified to take a job is now talking confidently of applying for an office job once she no longer needs to take care of her aged parents.

The woman who spent every day hiding from life now pulls back the drapes every morning, looks life in the eye, and says, "Now, what are we going to do together today?"

32

KAJ!

Kaj Nielsen was one of the most mysterious patients ever admitted to Hospital Vozandes-Quito.

One nurse was sure she had seen him two months before, in the eastern jungles of Ecuador. Looking up at him from a group of crying Indian babies, nursing mothers, and curious kids, she thought she saw the jaundiced skin and white-of-eye of infectious hepatitis even then. But he seemed more concerned about the health of his Shuar friends than about his own, she noticed vaguely. And he melted away before she had a chance to say anything. "Wonder what he's doing way out here?" But the thought only flickered through her mind. All sorts of white men co-habited with Indian women, and some men liked living in remote places.

Two months later he had turned up in Quito, at Vozandes Hospital, on an emergency flight from a little jungle village in the southeast of Ecuador on the other side of the Andes. The virus had done its worst: he was emaciated, his skin was sickly yellow, and his liver so inflamed and swollen that it was the size of a football, protruding through his abdomen. Kaj had walked alone for four days through the steamy equatorial rainforest to the closest village with a grass airstrip and a telephone, and called the Danish consul-general for help.

"In that condition!" Janet Anderson marveled as she looked down at the skeleton on the bed, the yellow skin, and that hugely protruding liver. Kaj's hair was long, dark, and tangled, and he certainly was not an Ecuadorian.

The prognosis wasn't good. The infectious hepatitis had raged unchecked through his body for months, and it was a particularly virulent strain. His liver was completely dysfunctional with advanced cirrhosis.

Kaj's only possession appeared to be a Danish passport which the consul-general explained he had issued to Kaj when he had presented himself at the Danish consulate in Quito several years before, asking for a new one. His old one was missing, Kaj had explained. His name was Kaj Nielsen, a crewman with a Danish shipping line. After ten years he wanted a stint at something else, and when his ship had berthed at Esmeraldas, it seemed as good a time as any. So the consulate had issued him a new Danish passport, and Kaj had disappeared.

Kaj might have been badly ill, but he was perfectly coherent and fluent. Not just in Danish, it turned out, but also in German, English, Spanish, and Shuar. Obviously linguistically gifted he spoke all five languages without trace of an accent.

After disembarking at Esmeraldas, Kaj told them, he had worked his way east through Ecuador, over the Andes, and down to the steamy Oriente—part of the huge catchment basin of the giant Amazon—where he lived with the local Shuar Indians and mended their simple machinery. Why on earth hadn't he come for treatment sooner? Kaj would never answer the question.

Hospital Vozandes-Quito is not an ordinary hospital. It was set up in 1955 as the caring arm of HCJB's radio service to America, its expatriate communities, and Europe. Station staff members decided that if they were trying to tell people God loved them, one of the best ways to demonstrate it was in the station's own back yard. So Hospital Vozandes-Quito started out as a small Indian clinic on the main highway just outside Quito, 9,300 feet up in the Andes, dispensing health care to the local community. As the radio network expanded, so did the hospital.

From 250 watts of power, the radio installation grew to more than one million watts, with a short-wave capability in twenty different languages and thirty dialects to Europe, Russia, Japan, Australia, New Zealand, and north and south through the Americas. The little clinic became two fully equipped hospitals

with a total eighty-five bed capacity (still under expansion)—
one in Quito and the other on the edge of the Amazon jungle—
not only treating and curing thousands of patients each year but
training Ecuadorians in basic health care and sending mobile
clinics to thousands of remote villagers each year by any means
possible: light aircraft, caravan, bus, canoe, and sometimes by
foot.

The philosophy behind the hospital paid off. Many patients
were familiar with the radio broadcasts, but it took the gentle
health care they received at Vozandes-Quito to reinforce the
message, and at the hospital they responded in their scores. The
experience of Ecuadorian chaplain, Jesús Montero, is not exactly
typical of a day's work, nor is it so far removed. He sat down not
so long ago with out-patients—Indians, mestizos, Spanish, and a
scattering of internationals—in the waiting room at Vozandes-
Quito at the start of the day. He quietly introduced himself, began to read passages from the Bible, and then discussed their
personal relevance. As he drew to a close, several patients asked
him to continue. By consensus he went on, and before clinic
opened that day fifteen patients had prayed quietly with him,
asking God to forgive them and change them. A different sort of
care.

So when Janet Anderson looked down at Kaj she wasn't as
concerned about his physical condition as she was about his refu-
sal to talk about his past. Something had obviously happened
that Kaj didn't plan to tell anyone about.

But the consul-general had been doing his own investiga-
tions, and he passed the information on to Hospital Vozandes-
Quito. Kaj Nielsen was a false name. Kaj's real name was
Johannes Brosig—a thirty-eight-year-old West German escapee
from a Danish prison. He was traveling under six different pass-
ports, but the only valid one was his West German passport. The
staff said nothing to Johannes Brosig.

Visiting him from day to day, Janet continued to call him
Kaj. Loving to play the guitar and sing, Janet, in a spontaneous
moment not long after she first met him, promised Kaj she would
bring her guitar in the following day and sing to him. As she sat

down and began singing in her light, clear voice, Kaj listened gratefully. As her eyes flickered to Kaj's face, Janet noticed that his brown, bloodshot eyes were filling with tears. As she sang on through "Lonely Voices," they overflowed down his gaunt cheeks. Janet put the guitar down quietly and wondered what to say to Kaj, then decided to tell him simply what she knew was true: that no matter what Kaj had done, God loved him and wanted to forgive him. Unsure how he would react, she half expected anger and bitterness, but Kaj wanted to hear more.

So a Swedish broadcaster, Iris, joined Janet on her visits— often two or three times a day—explaining carefully what God was like. Again and again they reassured him that God loved him and would forgive him; that it was not too late. Even so, they were startled when Kaj suddenly burst out: "Would God love someone who has killed somebody else?"

So that was it! "Yes," Janet responded instantly. "Like He forgave the thief on the cross." Kaj nodded his head.

But Kaj worsened steadily, lapsing into unconsciousness and beginning to vomit blood. Janet and Iris arranged for someone to be at his bedside night and day. On the first day, several people explained to Kaj how he could personally find God's forgiveness, but he did not respond.

Janet decided to speak to him herself. Leaning on the bed, she spoke quietly and slowly to Kaj: "Kaj, are you going to ask God to forgive you? Do you want to receive Jesus?" Kaj rolled his eyes, and Janet heard a weak but emphatic response, "Of course!" For the first time that day, Kaj was coherent. Trembling with weakness, he repeated after Janet a prayer asking for God's forgiveness and accepting the pardon. Then almost immediately he fell into a deep sleep.

There wasn't much evidence to go on, but Janet and Iris had got to know every feature of Kaj's emaciated face, and they noticed something that changed instantly. A small worried furrow on his forehead—his wrinkle of guilt, they used to call it— had gone. They never saw it reappear. But it was really all they had to go on, because Kaj was clearly dying. They continued talking quietly to him, reassuring him that God had forgiven him and loved him, and urging him to begin talking to his Father.

Early on a Sunday morning, three weeks after he had been admitted, Kaj died. The following day, the German broadcaster, Rüdiger Klaue, presided over a simple burial. Like the thief on the cross, he said, Kaj had made his appeal: "Jesus, remember me when You come into Your kingdom." And Jesus had replied: "Today you will be with Me in paradise."

33

REPUDIATED

Alton had sent his wife away—a common enough thing to do in traditional black Africa. Not that she had a disease, or was insane, or contentious—or even a bad cook. He'd sent her away because she had committed adultery—and few African men would have told him he'd done the wrong thing. He didn't get a decree nisi from the court; that's not the way it's done in black Africa. But as far as he was concerned, it was the end. He didn't want her back again, and she knew it.

There were no custody battles; the children stayed with him. Everyone knew she no longer had rights'to them. So Alton was living alone with his children when he switched on Radio Botswana one night for a bit of music. Instead he picked up Johanes Zwane in Swaziland on an English-language program called "Look and Live." Johanes was talking about forgiveness, and what he said had some effect on Alton, because not long after, Johanes received a 4" by 6" piece of note paper with a message in English written on one side.

"I pray that you remain there explaining the Bible untill [sic] you grow old and never be removed," Alton wrote. "The wife I divorced is with me now, thanking God and your explanation. I told her everything about your Bible study, and now she is interested in listening. Really God chose the right man to explain His word to His lost sheep."

That was all—and it was only when Alton was asked for more detail that he wrote again, saying that he was a black African who had grown up on Rhodesian black communal lands. His

father was a communal farmer, and he was one of a family of sixteen. He left school when he was twelve, and his boyhood wasn't
happy. "It was sad because there was injustice in the family,
caused by the Father." His parents were Seventh Day Adven-
tists, "and so were we all, but I never repented." His parents also
worshiped the spirits of their ancestors. He married a local girl—
"because I loved her"—but ten years later he sent her away for
adultery.

It's not clear how long they had been living apart when Alton picked up Johanes Zwane, but the message was loud and
clear—at least for Alton.

"Johanes was preaching about forgiveness of sins," Alton
explains, "and about forgiving our enemies and those who do
wrong to us, so that we may be sons of God." He quotes the Bible
reference he heard from Matthew 5:38-48:

> Do not take revenge on someone who wrongs you. If anyone
> slaps you on the right cheek, let him slap your left cheek too.
> And if someone takes you to court to sue you for your shirt, let
> him have your coat as well. And if one of the occupation
> troops forces you to carry his pack one kilometer, carry it two
> kilometers. . . .
>
> You have heard that it was said, Love your friends, hate your
> enemies. But now I tell you, love your enemies . . . so that
> you may become the sons of your Father in heaven. . . .

There was no doubt in Alton's mind who he had to love
and forgive—and not just to forgive but to try to be reconciled
with. "I *had* to go where she was staying," Alton says. "When I
found her, I told her, 'I am now a Christian, so God does not
want me to fail to forgive you—the wife of my youth.'"

His estranged wife was skeptical. "At first she did not believe me when I told her that, because she knew me as somebody
who had nothing to do with God's words," Alton says. "But I
told her that I have forgiven her all her mistakes and also I promised her not to talk about it any more when staying together, and

she finally agreed to come with me at once to her children at home."

Alton says he kept his promise not to rehearse the mistakes of the past, and it has paid off. "From the time I forgave her there was peace until now," he writes. "I have never spoken about it to her. Also my kids were very happy to see their mother back at home. And now she calls me 'Baba,'* something she never did before." He says she is listening with him to the programs and going with him to a church he has just joined.

He ends asking for prayer—"that I may overcome evil with good and also have a strong faith in Jesus every day until I go back to the dust where I was taken."

He signs off, "Yours in Christ, Alton Ndlovu."

---

* *Baba* means father and is a term of respect when used by a wife of her husband.

34
VOID

L ie awake at night and look up at the stars in deep space, then imagine that you're alone on this planet. It's enough to drive you to despair.

Jozef had often done that—lain down and looked up at the stars in the frozen wastes of space and imagined he was just an anonymous blob of human protoplasm, living and dying in an infinite void, on a planet that just happened—and an awful loneliness and despair would creep over him. That was why he'd come to a general conclusion that there had to be a God—and he'd come to it fairly early in life. But he lived in an atheist state. God didn't exist, they told him in the classroom. So he didn't know quite what to do about what he believed.

As a child he was thoughtful, quiet, and very observant. He asked a lot of questions and thought carefully and deeply about the answers. At thirty-three he hasn't changed. He's small and dark, quiet, alert, and deeply thoughtful—a geologist now, prospecting for minerals and raw materials in his country's rocky sub-strata. He's musical too—plays at least four instruments: the violin, saxophone, flute, and clarinet. He's been married one year, and his quick, blue eyes flicker appreciatively up as he says how helpful the broadcasts were while he was wondering how a believer in God should set about finding a wife.

He expresses himself precisely in his light tenor voice: "Even from my childhood I was interested in the universe— whether it was finite or infinite, whether it was created or just happened. I looked for order and meaning in life. I wanted to know, Is there a God or not? If there is, can men get to know Him or does He hide Himself? So I read a lot: literature about the universe and the laws of nature. I was very interested in the natural sciences."

By the age of twenty-three he was a regular listener to anything on radio that would tell him more about physics or the natural sciences. He also listened a lot to Radio Luxembourg, mainly for the music, and he was tuning up the station one night when he heard a voice in the Czech language. He hardly knew why he stopped and listened. "I think it was something about the voice," Jozef says. "Usually the voice of the announcer doesn't matter, but in this case it told me something. I tuned in carefully and listened very closely to this guy." At the end, the station identified itself—Trans World Radio, Monte Carlo.

He kept tuning in from time to time, and when he did, the old question resurfaced: Does God really exist? Sometimes the programs addressed a subject of particular interest to him, and it moved him. "It seemed that God, if He existed, was using other people to answer my questions, and that deeply affected me." So much so that Jozef decided to begin searching in earnest for the God he wanted to believe in.

He went to church. "It was the only church I knew of, and I went there several times, but I found nothing. I only felt something very lofty, which perhaps I could admire, something behind it all. Something Who must be. I talked to ordinary people, but when they spoke to me about God, they couldn't explain Him adequately or bring Him any closer to me. I found another church, and I went there, but it was the same. I received a lot of information, but nothing made God real or near."

Disappointed and busy at work, he stopped looking and no longer found time to listen to the programs. Then one day he was invited to a church he hadn't heard about before. This time it worked. "I was presented with a God who was alive and who I could believe in," he says.

Immediately he went back to his radio, found the programs, and from that point became a regular listener. "I made up my mind that I would make the true biblical view my own," he says. He was interested to find that the programs still seemed to be able to guess correctly the questions on his mind. "It made me realize again that God knew about me and was interested in me."

The faith and science programs reinforced what he was discovering for himself: harmony between science and the Bible. He regularly recorded them. The conflict he had been taught existed wasn't there as far as he could see. "For me the Bible only underlines what I read in science. I can believe in God because of the order and the uniqueness and the beauty I can see in nature."

But science wasn't all Jozef was interested in. As a man in his late twenties, he was looking around for the girl he should marry, and he learned a lot from the programs about the sort of wife he should seek. But the programs couldn't give her to him; he had to wait a bit for that. When she did come, however, he was amazed at the order, uniqueness, and beauty God added to His universe.

35
A CASE OF PRIORITIES

"**Y**ou can't love God and your bank balance. You can't keep on putting your job first—not all the time."

Jozef Kozak looks moodily out of the bus window, his light brown eyes perplexed. It's a bleak day in the capital. With his sleeve he rubs a clear patch on the window and peers out. It is raining now, the cloud is low, and the trees look stark and lonely without their leaves. The depressing day matches his state of mind.

The bus empties out. He buttons his coat against the fine, cold rain, tightens his grip on his briefcase, and heads at a run for the anonymous, gray state legal offices where he works as a law-yer—arguing with himself all the way. If he'd had a bit more courage, his colleagues would have known by now that he was a Christian. If he'd had a bit more courage, he would have gone to church and not cared if he'd lost his job.

The rain begins to sting his face, and he ducks into a hotel entrance for shelter. "A man has to live," he mutters to himself, his breath vaporizing in the air. "If I lose this job, what am I sup-posed to do? Dig? Anyway, why do I have to tell anyone any-thing? Can't they see for themselves?"

That had always been the conflict: keep quiet about what he believed and keep his job secure and his income safe, or make his convictions clear and risk being kicked out just at the point when he was about to qualify for a working-life's pension.

That was why he hadn't gone to church for more than four-teen years—he and Maria, his wife. They hadn't even mixed informally with Christians. You never knew who might report you—and then you might be "out."

But the words he'd heard on the radio a few days ago hammered against his conscience like the rain on the pavement. "No one can be a slave of two masters; he will hate one and love the other; he will be loyal to one and despise the other. You cannot serve God and money." That was the second or third time they'd come across that verse from the Bible, and now it wouldn't leave them alone!

The rain eases a little. Jozef takes a deep breath and bolts out of the shelter for the gray bulk of the state legal offices. One day soon, he promises himself as he forces open one of the large, double entrance doors, I'll resolve this conundrum.

Jozef had been a believer for more than fourteen years, but not as long as Maria. He hadn't been a believer when they married, though he'd had no objections when Maria told him that she believed in God and prayed. He used to pray too when he was a boy; as a man he'd given it up. But as he'd seen Maria praying, he had started to join her, and more and more often he listened with her to the radio. He'd become a believer himself through the programs. It was nothing in particular that he'd heard—he just believed one day, after he'd listened about four years, that Jesus Christ was God's son. After that the radio had been their only Christian company—especially after Maria's mother died. She was the only other Christian they'd seen regularly.

He and Maria had talked a lot about the problem. She was having the same struggle. She was a secondary school teacher. As professionals in an atheistic political system they had both hinted at a "better way" as much as they dared. Others had been bolder, they both knew that, but it was difficult to find the line between boldness and foolishness, wisdom and cowardice.

If they did make their positions clear, they stood to lose a lot: their income, their pension, their apartment (which wasn't luxurious), and the chances of finding another job. People who had jobs in this country—especially good jobs—made sure they kept them. They had both studied hard to get where they were.

She'd majored in history and geography at the Faculty of Mathematics and General Sciences. He had studied at the School of Law.

But as Jozef reached the legal offices that day, he was very close to making his decision. Others would have kept working and gone to church anyway. But Jozef and Maria were Jozef and Maria; they quieted their consciences their own way.

A few months later they both decided to stop work five years early. In their country that was a ridiculous thing to do; you kept working till you were pushed out because you needed every penny you could get. Jozef and Maria still had another five years of work ahead, five years of valuable income and pension increases. Going as early as they did, they knew they stood to lose out on one—or several—of the state's sudden, large, unannounced wage jumps, and a commensurate increase in their pensions. None of the West's carefully modulated wage rises here. Here wages could double overnight.

Jozef did take his courage in his hands before he retired. He started going to church a year before he resigned—a step that could have put his pension at risk and cost him his job, but it didn't. He retired at the age of fifty-five, five years before the compulsory male retiring age of sixty. Maria retired a year before him, at the age of fifty. Their combined pension in 1985 was $200 (American) a month.

Jozef the lawyer now keeps bees; Maria the teacher does a lot of reading, knitting, and embroidery. But only in their spare time. If you mention to Jozef that an aging arthritic believer faces a cold city winter in an apartment too expensive to heat, this tall, quiet, gray-moustachioed man with a liking for blue denim suits is likely to head for the nearest ax and spend the afternoon cutting and delivering wood—at no charge.

36

1 + 1 = 550

Mozambique—one of the unpolished gems of Africa: fertile and rich in mineral resources and bright young children with sparkling eyes and ebony skins.

Today Mozambique is shattered by war, its infant mortality rate one of the world's highest and its per capita income one of the world's lowest. Mozambique was one of the last African nations to throw off colonial rule. In September 1975, Portugal gave Mozambique her independence, and 250,000 whites trooped out with households and possessions, taking with them all their commercial and technological expertise, their aircraft, buses, and even their taxis. With a weary sigh, 400 years of Portuguese possession came to an end; the fires of African nationalism in the sixties and seventies had been too fierce for Portugal to resist. The Frelimo resistance movement in Mozambique had captured the aspirations of the people. For ten years Frelimo had carried on a guerrilla warfare, particularly in the north, operating at night or under cover of Mozambique's dense equatorial forest, laying mines and blowing up military convoys. But in 1974 it was all over. The "gentle revolution" in Portugal installed a military junta determined to shed its overseas possessions, and Portugal, by then the poorest nation in Western Europe, handed over the reins of Mozambique power to Frelimo.

Predictably, Frelimo's struggle had been exploited by the power blocs, so it was not surprising to find a black communist dictator at the helm. Streets were given communist names, farms were regrouped into state communes, schools and hospitals were nationalized, and religion was banned—especially the religion of the old colonial regime.

Then the backlash started. Embittered Portuguese and whites, backed by South Africa, struck back to ensure that no black communist government succeeded. Mercenaries swelled the ranks, and the movement gave itself a name—the Mozambique National Resistance—though the locals knew them better as *bandidos*. So the war in Mozambique continued. But now it was a crueler, more vicious war, and its sole aim was to cripple the regime and lay waste the economy.

By 1985 the *bandidos* dominated the northern half of Mozambique and were reaching south. They would swoop in unannounced, bombing, burning, and looting whole villages, killing, mutilating, and taking slaves. Their special targets were industrial plants, schools, and hospitals. As terrorized rural populations fled to towns, agricultural production plummeted, worsened by drought. Famine followed. By 1986 one-hundred-thousand people had been killed by the *bandidos*, and the livelihood of thousands of others destroyed. By 1987 literacy had plummeted to 13 percent, 2 million people had been displaced, and one third of the country's health network and twenty-six hundred of its primary schools had been destroyed. Shops were empty, exports had fallen by two thirds, and the beleaguered Frelimo government was spending almost half its budget on the war effort. By 1988 international relief agencies were calling for food for 6.5 million people, almost half the Mozambican population. By then the country had the lowest per capita income in the world.

Mozambique 1989: broken by war and famine, hopeless and poverty-stricken, its economic infrastructure in ruins. People everywhere were looking for meaning in a mindless war, for comfort and personal significance. As if in concession, the government backed away from some of its socialist dogma and admitted that its blanket ban on religion had been ill advised. Churches began to reopen, and many of them had standing room only. In Montepuez in the far north, where war had been a fact of life for more than twenty years, Juma's church had already spilled out the doors and into nine other towns.

Juma was in his teens when Portugal gave Mozambique its independence, and in its small compound of circular mud huts, his family breathed a sigh of relief at the promise of an end to the fighting. Juma was a Yao, one of a black Muslim tribe. Like everyone else in the region who had a radio, he could pick up the Chinese propaganda broadcasts from Dar-es-Salaam over the border in Tanzania. One evening he flicked the switch on his father's old Mbili Soba Saba transistor and found himself tuned into a Swahili program—"Nono La Uzima" ("Words of Life"), then "Biblia Inajibu" ("Answers from the Bible").

Interesting! But as a Muslim he was puzzled by the references to Jesus Christ, the Son of God—it was an outrageous blasphemy that Allah would procreate with a another man's wife. But he was curious to know more and listened regularly for several years.

Juma was training as a technician at the time, but his studies ground to a halt with the onset of a painful neuralgia. His cousin took him to a witchdoctor in Tanzania, who told him too much study was hurting his head. Juma was highly skeptical but, spurred by the programs he was hearing, decided to switch his field of study to Islam. He stayed in Tanzania studying the Koran with the local *Madrasas* (teachers) and listening to the broadcasts. Then, on a Portuguese program "Palavras de Vida" ("Words of Life"), there it was again: believe in the Son of God, and you will be saved. Confused, Juma sought out a fellow Mozambican, Rev. Muito, a tribal Makonde, now a Christian.

Rev. Muito knew the Koran, and he knew Juma's native Swahili. They discussed the Koran together, and Rev. Muito invited Juma to church. Juma says only that the sermon and prayer that day were "a great lesson." They had enough in common with the radio broadcasts that Juma began to attend the church regularly, and at the same time the attacks of neuralgia stopped.

It was seven years before Juma returned to Montepuez. It was 1985, and the Frelimo government was fighting a losing battle against the *bandidos*, who were entrenched around Montepuez and were extending south. People were curious: Juma had left a Muslim and returned a Christian. Juma wasted no time explaining, and it wasn't long before a group of people was meeting in his house—a simple hut with thatched roof and earthen walls. So began the Church of Christ in Montepuez, and it grew by leaps and bounds.

Within several years Juma's church was two hundred strong, cascading out of his hut and reproducing itself all around the district: at Napela, three miles from Montepuez; at Nacuca, twenty-five miles away; at Patampandane, 110 miles away; at Mueda, 250 miles to the north. By the end of 1988, 550 people were meeting in nine churches and listening together to FEBC, Seychelles.

Juma's story came to light through a letter that arrived out of the blue at FEBC's offices. "I thank God I can write to you," he says. "I am full of the riches of Christ. I want you to know that I have given the gospel of the Lord Jesus to our community, and we have more than two hundred believers. We are a very young church—we are not walking yet, still crawling. We are starting to build a house of prayer—a hut with grass on it, but at the moment we are meeting in the house of a man who loves God. We are in the [war zone] where everything is difficult for us, but we are working happily towards the Kingdom of God. Please pray for us."

Juma has had very little formal training. But he's managing. "Everything I know has come from the radio," he says. "I listen all the time." In a country like Mozambique—where even batteries are scarce—that's not an easy thing to do.

37

A MATTER OF EXPLOSIVES

"**I** want you to help me because I want to desert so I can turn my life over completely to your Christ, who I have longed to have in my life for years. I am tired of fighting for a cause that gives me only remorse and nauseates me. If I don't find God I am going to kill myself with my rifle."

The sentence was part of a letter that arrived early in 1984 in the office of a team of radio programmers working out of a Latin American country:

"Jungle"
February 27, 1984
4:50 A.M.

"Dear Pastor,

"I am writing to congratulate you on your marvelous program. I always listen to you on short wave even though I don't belong to your religion. We can hear you clearly in this part of the jungle.

"This is why I am writing to you. I've known the message of the Holy Bible for about 14 years but I haven't had the chance to get better acquainted with it because I have to spend so much of my time on watch. We are guerrillas.

"My speciality is explosives and right now I'm 40 feet off the ground in a tree, surrounded by sleeping monkeys, my Russian grenades, my US-made rifle, and other arms. It's a beautiful jungle spot, everything is quiet and clear, and we are waiting for a brilliant sunrise.

"It's because of your programs that I'm about to do what I am: finish completely with this way of life, which I now count as lost time. If I don't hurry to find out what the truth is, I know I will be totally destroyed physically and spiritually.

"Besides being a subversive person I am also a chronic drug addict and a lover of social corruption. I'm possessed by a demon of sexual mania and slavery and much more I'm too ashamed to tell you about. Pastor, please help me because I don't think I am a normal man; I think I'm a son of the Devil, and that's the cause of my problems. I don't think God is interested in forgiving me for all I have done over these long bad years.

"I thought that I was free. No one on the face of the earth was ever going to tell me that I was a sinner. I thought I would never die because in all my fighting in this country and others, I have never been wounded. But I have to say that I am afraid of dying. I am very much afraid. Right now I am surrounded by 60 pounds of powerful explosives that at any moment could destroy me.

"Today I am going to go to the city to mail this letter; in fact, I have enough money to travel to the capital so that I can mail the letter to you from there.

"It is now 5:38 A.M., and I'm going to abandon my monkeys, my grenades, my rifle, and everything to do with my life as a guerrilla, but I am taking two Bibles with me."

Tucked into the same letter that arrived that February morning was a brief note:

"Jungle City."
7:02 A.M.

"Dear Pastor,

"In 30 minutes I leave for the capital city. I already have my ticket. A friend traveling with me is going to say that I'm a member of his family so that no one will suspect I'm a guerrilla. But I'm scared to death, and my nerves are screaming.

"I have prayed the short prayer that I learned through your radio program and am asking God to protect me and help me get out safely.

"Please don't tell anyone what I have told you, unless they believe as you do, because I don't want anyone to know about this until God has saved me and I know it.

"Please don't reject me as others have done. I've asked others for help and got none. My safety depends on you because now both the military and the revolutionaries will be after me. Please help me because I'm terribly afraid.

"Well—the hour has come to travel towards a new life.

Your friend, Juan Carlos."

Juan Carlos Ocampo Quintero was twenty-seven years old when he penned his first letter from the heart of a jungle somewhere in Latin America.

He was the "commander" of a guerrilla detachment trained by communist partisans. His philosophy was atheistic. His cache of weapons came from international communism and North American arms manufacturer. A rival guerrilla group had killed his wife—also a terrorist—and his eleven-year-old son was living in the capital city with his grandfather.

The "friend" he mentioned in his note was a pilot, and Juan Carlos had bribed him with a large amount of money, not his own, to tell anyone who asked that he was a relative. He flew out sharing a cabin with men under government orders to find and wipe out centers of guerrilla resistance.

When he arrived in the capital Juan Carlos posted his letter, and it arrived at its destination the following evening. A counselor with the team replied immediately, and there was a nervous wait for further word: insincere contacts from enemies of the state were a risk. But Juan wrote again—a month later, April 1984—from the capital city.

"Warmest greetings to all the members of the evangelistic team. I got your letter and understood what you said very clearly. I went to the evangelical church to receive Christ as my personal

Savior, and that's what I did. I want you to know that I have totally changed and have the peace in my soul that I was searching
for.

"I wasn't able to get back to you sooner because my former
comrades are hunting me, and also, of course, the military. How
I thank God He snatched me from my lost condition.

"Would you send me a small commentary on the Bible, and
a concordance? Please pray for me. I'm between the sword and
the wall, though I know God will help me. My greatest desire is
to be a faithful worker for Christ.

"I hope to get to you soon so I can tell you all about it."

Over a period of about twelve months Juan Carlos wrote
seventeen letters to the broadcasters in his flourishing hand. He
also turned his pen to other kinds of prose: he wrote a paper,
"How to Pray and Be Heard by God," and dedicated "this small
and insignificant study, to the Person Who has been interested
in my soul, spirit, life, and well-being on this earth from the cre-
ation of the world. There aren't enough words to say what this
powerful Person Whom I love has done in my life." An excerpt
reads: "Dear brother, remember that prayer is the greatest of all
weapons—even greater than an M-16 rifle or a fragmentation
grenade." He also wrote other papers: "Why Be a Christian?";
"My Decision to Serve God"; and "Who Is God?"

But increasingly his letters began to talk of growing personal danger, and he left the city where he attended church for a
much larger church in another city. One of his pastors recalls
seeing changes in the former guerrilla: "he became a less demanding and more patient individual."

His last letter was dated May 1985, and the sudden stop to a
steady and lively correspondence was ominous. In the letter he
was worried that his elderly father was probably putting his life
on the line by giving him asylum.

As the months passed there was still no word, and rumors
began to circulate: he had been killed, or he had returned to ter-
rorism, or he had gone back to his group to tell them about the
"powerful Person" who had changed his life.

But no one *knew* what had happened.

After eighteen months the team tried to track him down but met only dead ends. The radio pastor who answered Juan Carlos's first letter, and who remained a close confidant and advisor, knew most.

He said that Juan Carlos's son had been shot and killed —almost certainly by members of Juan Carlos's former band. Certainly the killers were members of an extreme left-wing revolutionary group financed by communism and drug money, and among the most violent in the country. They also made two attempts on Juan Carlos's life, and in the second, shrapnel from a hand grenade lobbed at him in a city café inflicted injuries.

Only shortly after the incident Juan Carlos had come to tell his pastor that he was going back to the jungles to tell his former comrades about Jesus Christ. Nothing more has been heard of Juan. If he was still alive, there would certainly have been word from him; he was such a regular writer. The best guess is that he did exactly what he told the pastor he would do: he returned to his comrades—the ones who had killed his son and tried twice to kill him—to tell them that God could forgive them too and change them. He almost certainly went unarmed because he told the pastor he wanted his only weapon to be the Bible.

Juan's friends believe he is dead. If he is, his only epitaph will be that written in heaven: "A grain of wheat remains no more than a single grain unless it is dropped into the ground and dies. If it does die, then it produces many grains."

38
CHAIN REACTION

They troop into the room—three generations of women elegantly wrapped in bright saris—testimony to the impossible: survival in an Indian city rush hour.

Somehow Phillips did it—dodged his pretty party around lumbering oxcarts, pushy little moto-shaws, taxis, brimming buses, overladen trucks, wandering cows, stray pedestrians, and potholes as deep as craters, through swarms of sidewalk vendors and the colorful, smoky clamor and chaos of early morning Hyderabad—without disturbing a hair or unraveling a sari. Negotiating the streets of Hyderabad in rush hour is obviously something Phillips does every day.

Phillips isn't as elegant as his bevy; he hasn't shaved for a couple of days, and you don't expect to see the bare feet showing under his neatly pressed shirt and trousers. But that's Phillips, and Phillips has a grin as wide as the spread of his bare, brown feet as he introduces his family and tells how it happened.

"It was a kind of chain reaction," he says, and points to the members of the family in turn. "First, it was my sister, then me, then my wife, then my mother, then my sister's husband and little girl, and then my other brother and sisters." It starts getting complicated, and they're not sure of the order anyway.

But what *was* certain was that "Vishwa Vani"* started it all and had a good hand in everything else that happened. And it was all because Phillip's sister, Arogya Mary, was married to a

---

* Trans World Radio's Indian partner.

man who was a fan of India's popular film music and because he turned on the radio one day to a station that played it a lot. As he fine-tuned the radio he found himself very close to another station, broadcasting something in the Telegu language that he'd never heard before.

"Mary," he shouted, "come and listen to this!" Mary came and heard just enough to decide she didn't want to hear any more. Someone was talking about Jesus Christ, but Arogya Mary had been named after the Virgin, and Mary didn't hear a word about the Virgin, so she didn't listen long. Her husband stayed tuned a little longer, then went back to his film music.

A week later, he caught the edge of the same "Vishwa Vani" program again. This time he listened right through and found the program was a daily regular. He decided to listen every day, and Arogya Mary thought she might listen too—but just to the songs, not to anything anybody said. Except that one day she did listen, and it was a bit from the Bible about Jesus Christ standing at the door knocking and why didn't she open the door? It made her curious, and she began to wonder what was in the Bible. But no Bible was in the house, so she did nothing about it until her daughter suddenly brought one home from school—a gift from the Gideons.

She began to listen more often. Usually the programmers said, "Open your Bible and read with us. . . ." So she started doing that, and one evening the program took a look at a certain passage: "If we say we have no sin, we deceive ourselves, but if we confess our sins to God . . . He will forgive us."

Arogya Mary is plump and bespectacled and in her thirties, her long, black hair drawn tightly back from her round face. "I couldn't get around that verse, 'How can I say I am not a sinner,'" she says. "I told lies, I used bad language, I lived for myself, I wanted more money, and more and better everything—clothes, jewelry." She felt she needed to do something about what she'd heard, so she turned the radio off and began to pray—just a small prayer, asking God to forgive her.

Three hours later she was still praying. The small prayer opened a floodgate, and for half an hour it seemed her whole life's misdeeds spilled in front of her. A childhood memory came vividly alive—Arogya Mary lacing the tea with kerosene before her sister sold it to customers at their tea house. But Arogya Mary cleaned up the record with God that night, and at the end of the three hours she was so happy she couldn't find words to express herself. "I told the family what had happened and that they had to listen to the programs," she says.

But Phillips and his mother decided that they had no intention of being bitten by whatever had got hold of Arogya Mary. They were all right: the family had been Roman Catholic for generations; they went to Mass, and prayed to Mary, St. Xavier, and St. Anthony. They invented a couple of new names for Arogya Mary—"Preacher" and "Bible Woman."

Certainly Phillips didn't plan to listen to "Vishwa Vani." He went to Mass for ten minutes each week and was confident that would get him through the final judgment. In the meantime heaven had nothing much to do with life down here, and at twenty-three Phillips was busy living—and having a hard time staying sober and out of trouble.

He was a messenger boy at the national bank, and it was probably only because he wasn't dealing with the public that they put up with his drunkenness on the job. Sobriety was difficult on three or four bottles of rum a day. He was also chain smoking—six to seven packs a day—lying if he could get a few rupees out of it, and spending a lot of his nights down at the girls' college. His parents finally decided to get him married to settle him down a bit, and they found a nice, quiet, Roman Catholic girl for him—which changed nothing.

But not everything Arogya Mary had said to Phillips had fallen on deaf ears, and although Phillips never tuned in to a "Vishwa Vani" broadcast deliberately, he did do it accidentally one night when he switched on the radio to hear some film music. He didn't hear much—just enough to ruffle him slightly. It was a song—"When Jesus comes He will give His reward"— about death, a final accounting, and rewards and penalties. He mentioned it casually to Arogya Mary: "What's this thing about rewards? Is Jesus going to give me a reward?"

Arogya Mary was in like a shot. "You don't stand a chance," she said. "There aren't any rewards for ten minutes of

Mass on Sundays. No rewards unless you get to heaven first, and you're nowhere near. You've got to confess your sins to Jesus and be saved, or God's just going to have to leave you in darkest night."

Phillips spent a restless night. When he woke up as usual at 3:30 A.M., he switched on the radio and found he was tuned into another "Vishwa Vani" program. This one wasn't in Telegu, it was in Bengali, but he knew enough to understand the quotes from the Bible, and it just repeated what Arogya Mary had said the previous night. Phillips was scared. He decided to do what they said—say he was sorry to God and clean up his act. He meant it, and he was surprised at a sudden lightening of spirit and sense of well being.

He decided he'd better stop his nocturnal visits to the girls' college, but he still drank and couldn't see anything wrong with seven packs of cigarettes a day, until a month later a sudden severe pain stabbed his chest while he was listening to a program about the narrow way that leads to life and the broad way that leads to death. It was enough to change his mind. So he kicked the nicotine and the alcohol, and the change didn't escape the staff at the bank. Nor was Phillips slow to account for it. They laughed at him, just as he had laughed at Arogya Mary, but watched with interest, nevertheless, as his habits and language continued to clean up—and did their best to ignore him when he began handing out "Vishwa Vani" program schedules.

His young wife, Ludh Mary, saw the 180-degree turn and could hardly believe it. She began to listen with Phillips to the programs. She thought she didn't have anything to apologize to God about; she hadn't lived like Phillips. But Phillips, Arogya Mary, and the programs had another line: God doesn't accept you just because you're good.

Ludh Mary is a quiet, attractive girl with a toddler on her knee. "It took me a while to accept that I was no more acceptable to God than Phillips had been," she says, "that even my best wasn't good enough." But she capitulated, finally, with a sense of relief and a prayer asking for God's forgiveness and a new life.

And then it was grandmother's turn. She'd watched what had been happening to Arogya Mary with pity, to Phillips with amazement, and now to Ludh Mary with bewilderment. She needed help herself with a drinking problem, and the kids kept saying that if she wanted it, she should listen to the broadcasts. So she did, but it was a book Arogya Mary gave her that meant most. Above all the other lines of print one passage stood out—a Bible verse: "Whoever loves me will obey my teaching . . . and my Father and I will come to him and live with him." Grandmother is small and lean and wrinkled. "I was forced into a corner," she says. "If I wanted God's help I had to obey Jesus' teaching." So she asked God to help her do it and apologized for living without Him.

Arogya Mary's husband wasn't far behind. He was listening to "Vishwa Vani" regularly and could see for himself what was happening in his wife's family. He finally added himself to their number at about the same time as his daughter, Mary Frederick, decided to as well—at Sunday school. Phillips's two other sisters and a brother have since joined them—but the remaining brother keeps a watchful distance.

They're not a family to keep quiet about what has happened. Arogya Mary and Phillips go most places armed with "Vishwa Vani" broadcast schedules and an evangelistic vocabulary. Grandmother is also on the warpath. "Well, if you won't listen to me, listen to 'Vishwa Vani,'" she tells people.

These days Phillips never goes anywhere without his Bible and a badge on his lapel. Today's button says, "Smile, Jesus loves you." Phillips doesn't believe in advertising anything he hasn't tried himself, and he's doing a lot of smiling these days—usually through at least a week's growth of beard.

39
OBNOXIOUS

You can almost hear the man from Inner Mongolia spluttering as he tries to find the words to describe the man he used to be, and he comes up with more than a couple: perverse, ignorant, narrow-minded, pig-headed, manipulative, deceitful, self-indulgent, unfaithful, contemptuous, always right about everything. Not surprising, perhaps, that his home life was in tatters and his colleagues and even his brothers and sisters thought he was obnoxious.

Though people disliked and avoided him, he could never see it. He lashed out at his wife and kids whenever his quick temper flared, and sometimes he beat them. He and his wife were always fighting. Even when she suddenly divorced him in November 1982 the truth didn't really start to come home; not even when his eldest son refused to live with him any longer and took off as well.

But eight months later something was starting to get through. He was depressed and confused, and a lot of things were getting on his nerves—even the radio, which he had on a lot of the time. But he had it on one July day, and he heard a clear voice saying, "Come to me all you who are weary and heavily laden, and I will give you rest." Curious, he listened more closely, then tuned in the following day. Some more words stuck: "Christ is the Way, the Truth, and the Life. Come to Him. Turn away from your own ways, and believe in Him. God rewards good and punishes evil."

As he kept listening he began to see himself in another light, and after four months he was shattered. "I really saw myself as I was. I was monstrous," he wrote to the broadcaster he had heard. "I just felt totally lost. I finally knelt down before God, and I prayed." Uncertain whether his prayer had been acceptable, he told the broadcaster exactly what he had prayed:

"'O Lord, I'm not just a sinner, I'm one of the worst of the lot. I admit it. I believe You are Christ, God's only Son and that You came to earth to rescue us. I believe You rose from the dead after they nailed You on the cross. When You rose from the dead You gave new hope and life to those who believed in You. I believe You are the Savior. I believe You are the true God and that You will reward those who search for You. O God, please accept me.'

"Do you think this prayer was OK? Do you think Jesus will accept me?" Regardless, the prayer marked a new beginning, he said. "I listen to you every day, and my mind is beginning to change. It's true, isn't it? God does have special divine power— supernatural power and love. There's nothing else that can change your heart, is there?"

He writes about growing happiness and peace of mind and improving health, though "things haven't been easy since I started to believe in God." He had a better attitude toward work. At home he was managing the household, looking after the kids better, and bit by bit people were seeing a different man. "My eldest son has come back home again, and my relationship with the children is quite different," he says. "My relatives no longer despise me. At work they're no longer trying to avoid me. They're treating me as if I'm a different person. But I *am* a different person. What Christ says is true, 'When any man is joined to Christ he is a new person; the old is gone and the new has come.'"

Lau says there are no Christians near him and certainly no pastor or church. He doesn't have a Bible, so he asks the broadcasters to pray he will be able to buy one somehow, somewhere. He wants to be baptized but realizes that's just about impossible. "Am I allowed to call myself a Christian if I haven't been baptized?" he asks. "Please write and tell me."

He wants to repay God somehow for what has happened to him, but doesn't know how, except to send money to the broadcasters to help pay for the programs he hears. "You guided me to God, thanks and praise be to Him. Listening to His words and following Him are ways of repaying Him I know, but for me it's not enough." And he signs off: "Now may the blessing of God be with you."

Alberto Gómez and Pedro
Ecuador

HCJB

40
PEDRO AND THE CONGRESSMAN

"The best laid plans of mice and men oft go astray," penned a celebrated Scottish bard, Robert Burns, in the eighteenth century. Liberally rephrased to fit a contemporary situation, this saying could run, "That was one bill the Quito Congress never passed in the fifties."

Politics in Ecuador has always been turbulent: the country's post-colonial history is a pageant of infighting, war, military coups, and popular revolts. Stable periods did occur, but they were few and far between, and even then *Politica* was a dirty word. One of Ecuador's more stable periods occurred in the postwar years with the boom in banana exports, and it is in this era that our story takes place, on a hacienda high in the Ecuadorian Sierra—the Andean highlands.

The hacienda owners—patrons—in the Sierra's mountain basins are economically powerful, upper class, and politically very influential. Their estates are often vast production centers of grains, fruits, and vegetables for the domestic market. Patrons today are the heirs of the *encomienda* system, introduced by the Spaniards in the sixteenth century, a system that reduced the local Quechua Indian populations to servitude. The Quechua have labored on the haciendas, impoverished, illiterate, and unskilled, without voting rights, speaking in their own tongue, and giving their labor in exchange for a small plot of private land, a subsistence wage, and an adobe hut with a thatched roof and the floor for a bed.

Today the Quechua are being schooled and taught Spanish, and the franchise has been extended to all literate citizens. Agrarian reform is releasing them from the haciendas, but Quechua Indians still remain an isolated group, largely living at subsistence levels away from the national urban centers and often addicted to chicha, a liquor made from chewed maize mixed with spittle. A fiesta, any celebration, even a small household event, is an excuse to drink chicha, and Indians will be drunk for days at a time. On the haciendas it was no different. The meager wage the Quechua workers did earn was spent on chicha, so the cycle of poverty continued.

The Quechua Indians who presented themselves at Alberto Carlos Gómez's stately *casa de hacienda* that day were hacienda workers. It was Pedro, his family, and friends. They had trooped up the vast staircase to the balcony and knocked on the door.

Alberto Gómez had a guest that day, and as they had been sitting and chatting on the balcony, groups of workers straggled past below them to the village saloon. It was a Sunday, and most of the workers would spend all they had. "Off to get drunk again, I see," Don Alberto's friend remarked. Don Alberto had barely answered, "Sí," when Pedro knocked at the door.

"Patron, may we come in and hear your wonderful box that sings and speaks?" Pedro appealed.

"Sí, sí, Pedro," said Don Alberto. "Come in, and I'll start it for you."

The entourage trooped in, sat on the floor, and listened so intently that they barely noticed Don Alberto's guest watching them with some interest. Program over, Pedro and friends left.

Don Alberto's guest wandered out on to the balcony, watching them, then suddenly started down the steps. Keeping his distance he followed Pedro and his party and noticed that they didn't go to the village saloon. He watched them to their huts and saw they were clean and tidy. The children were neatly dressed. He returned to Don Alberto, deeply thoughtful. "They didn't go to the saloon!" The surprise was evident in his voice. "Why are they so different from the others?"

Don Alberto shrugged. "Yes, they are different, but don't ask me why. They're always here wanting to listen to 'Voice of the Andes.' If that's what's doing it, I wish more would listen."

Don Alberto's friend was silent. When he left the hacienda on Monday morning and returned to Quito, he knew what he was going to do. A conservative congressman, he was going to lobby hard to throw out the bill now before Congress that would terminate foreign ownership or operation of any newspaper or radio station in Ecuador—a bill that meant the end of HCJB, the "Voice of the Andes," if it were passed. Back in Quito he told his colleagues what he had seen on the hacienda, and gradually a voting majority gathered around him. When the bill finally came to the vote, it was thrown out.

Missionaries with HCJB had begun praying immediately when they heard the bill was before Congress. In their minds there is every connection between their prayers and the congressman's visit to the hacienda in the Sierra on the same weekend that Pedro knocked on the door.

EPILOGUE:
ORIGINS AND EXPLANATIONS

No one asked me to write this book; I certainly wasn't com-missioned. I didn't even volunteer. Let's say I was pushed.

It's even unfair to say I wrote it—let's say *we* wrote it. I couldn't have written a word if Neil hadn't put me (often more literally *shoved* me) for seven months onto the planes and trains that took me where I had to go. Neil is my husband and my best friend, and without him the idea would never have got off the ground. He became my manager—not because I am totally in-competent but because he likes managing. He's not actually a manager. He's a nuclear chemist, but he knows his way so well around the atom that the world's easy.

I'm a journalist, with a background of twelve years in print journalism in New Zealand, Downunder. As I've already indicat-ed, this book happened to me rather unexpectedly and only be-cause Neil applied for a research job at a United Nations International Atomic Energy Agency laboratory in Monaco on the French Riviera. (The UN has its labs in the nicest places.) He got the job, and we packed a few bits and pieces, joined hands, flew 20,000 kilometers, and arrived in Monaco on a bril-liantly clear winter's day in 1984. We rented a floor in a fur-nished villa in a small French village, bought a beat-up old Honda, and Neil started his four-year contract while I wandered round with a dictionary and an elementary *oui et non* grasp of the language, wondering what to do with myself.

Enter Trans World Radio, the topic of this book.

Trans World Radio (TWR) is an interesting animal. It began as a one-lung affair on a 2500-watt transmitter in Tangier in 1954—and just kept growing, until today it's an international organization with hundreds of staff of scores of nationalities, more than five million watts of transmission strength, a multi-million dollar budget (financed from voluntary contributions), and millions of listeners during any twenty-four-hour period. At least one of the eighty or so languages in which it broadcasts can be heard almost anywhere on the globe at some time of the day or night. The languages are different, but the listeners are all getting basically the same message from hundreds of different speakers.

One of TWR's seven stations is right on the French Mediterranean, near Italy, and I wandered into the Monaco studios to see if I could be of any help. I was given PR work to do, on the writing side, but the work was hardly engrossing, and I was about to quietly disappear from the scene when a member of the staff happened to make a casual comment one day: "What we really need is a book of radio stories." Almost throw-away words, but they wouldn't leave me alone. They bugged me all day and most of the night as well. I kept waking up and lying awake for ages, while a voice in the back of my head kept saying, "You could do this, you know!" Nothing would stifle it, so I was finally forced to take it seriously.

Which is how it all started, and once you've sent out a hundred letters to stations, national offices, and broadcasters, it's hard to pull out. And I could have been tempted to, because it soon became clear that I was going to have to do all of the interviewing myself; no one else on staff had the time to do it for me, even if they had had the inclination, though there was a huge amount of goodwill. Nor did TWR have a policy about people like me, and I wasn't going to wait around till one evolved in boardrooms. The idea had picked me up by the scruff of the neck and wouldn't put me down; so what could I do? And Neil said he would finance the research. (God bless the UN.) So, after only one interview turned up on cassette in response to my letters, I did the next obvious thing: told staff I was coming and gave them

enough advance warning to do something about it. The reason-
ing was simple: flesh and blood on the doorstep is a lot harder to
put in a nonurgent file than is a letter.

So I hefted a large blue pack on my back, bought myself a
new reporter's cassette recorder, and traveled around Europe for
three months talking to listeners in Yugoslavia, Czechoslovakia,
Hungary, Germany, Spain, Belgium, Italy, France, and England. Then, what I call the Marathon began: a four-months'
tour through South America, India, and the Middle East—albeit
broken by several weeks in New Zealand with Neil for Christmas. Asia and Africa were left off the itinerary; Orientals rarely
open up to each other, let alone to Westerners carrying cassette
recorders, and I was advised Africa was too vast and dangerous.
So I just kept on hoping that enough Chinese and African listeners would get inspired to write long letters to broadcasters and
that somehow the broadcasters and I would find each other.

I spent the last half-hour before the Marathon soaking
Neil's shoulder with hot tears. My imagination, barely under
control at the best of times, had this time exceeded all limits. I
was half convinced I would never return alive. My itinerary took
me through Venezuela, Brazil, Uruguay, Argentina, Sri Lanka,
India, Egypt, Jordan, Israel, and Turkey. I could already see myself coming down with dysentery, yellow fever, malaria, typhoid,
and hepatitis, all at once, on a dirty riverboat up the Amazon. I
could just about feel the giant jaws of some beady-eyed crocodile
closing around me, or the vicious teeth of a school of piranha
tearing at my flesh as a canoe overturned, or an anaconda drop-
ping out of a tree and strangling me to death. I half expected to
become a leper. I imagined myself lying on the ground in some
seedy quarter beaten, raped, and robbed of passport and money,
and the stories I had heard about vicious interrogations, kidnap,
and murder by taxi-drivers, hotel proprietors, bogus officials, and
even one's new-found friends had turned my knees to water.

But through it all the voice in the back of my head said
from time to time, "You can do this, you know," and I thought
that if I was going to die I may as well do it gloriously. I had the
words of the apostle Paul to comfort me: "On many journeys I
have been in perils from rivers, from robbers, in the city, in the

wilderness, in the sea—in danger of death many times." If the great apostle had such a sanguine attitude about his personal safety, how could I be any less confident? So I left the villa in France for the flight to Venezuela, repeating the battle cry of a queen of old, "If I perish, I perish," and Neil sang hymns all the way to the airport.

Well, I wasn't beaten, robbed, raped, or tortured. The closest I came to death was dysentery and self-administered last rites during a violently bumpy flight in an overloaded aircraft flying without instruments over the jungle of the Brazilian interior in a tropical storm. I was almost trapped for a week in a remote jungle town with only enough money for a one-night stay, and I had a couple of scary flooded river crossings in pencil-thin canoes, but only one person tried asking me for a bribe. And I'd faced more theft attempts on Italian trains than I met anywhere on the Marathon. And as for leprosy—there's not a sign, though I regularly look behind my ears for red, flaky spots.

I returned to Monaco the day before our wedding anniversary and almost fell asleep during our special celebration dinner the following night. When I counted all the tapes I had there were ninety, and it was time to start transcribing them to paper. They were stories of murderers, alcoholics, guerrillas, lepers, the suicidal, the old and lonely and the not so old and lonely, the religious, the sick, the blind, the young and aimless, widows, and a whole lot of decent, ordinary, middle-class folks; also featured were a millionaire, a Hindu Sadhu, an unmarried mother, a scientist, the rich and wretched, the poverty-stricken, sufferers from nervous tension, guilt, hate, compulsive stealing, broken marriages, incest, and grief; others included the superstitious, witchcraft workers, the demon-possessed, the drug-dependent, the persecuted, the fearful, the depressed, the bitter, the timid, the hopeless, the self-righteous, the sorrowful. There were the plain miraculous: How *did* that lost, battered, light aircraft, almost out of fuel and with no communications antennae, still manage to limp home on a radio directional finder, fine tuned to a TWR program? Some people heard voices, dreamed dreams, saw visions in connection with programs; others just made a quiet U-turn.

But basically they all told me the same thing, regardless of country, customs, upbringing, standard of living, or how well or badly life had treated them. They said they had experienced God tangibly, through a voice out of a little rectangular box—in the kitchen, in a hammock, out in the desert or the jungle or the fields, in their bedrooms, in lounges, at bus-stops, in buses, in taxis, at sea. What they had experienced differed from person to person, but in every case it was radically life changing, and in essence they said, "Once I was blind, now I see."

They were new, restored people now, and they could laugh about it—sometimes through their sorrow, sometimes freely. Some of them cried. None told his or her story without emotion. They said chains had fallen off inside, and they were free. Of what? Many things: fear, revenge, unforgiveness, addictions, compulsions. And as a result marriages were patched up, kids behaved better, work situations improved, hope replaced hopelessness. They had really discovered Someone who deeply cared and was willing to clean up their lives and live with them—forever.

The listeners were often simple people who had no reason to lie to me; they just told it like it was. And I sat there, running with perspiration or shivering with cold, depending on the altitude or latitude, while they poured it all into my interpreter, who poured it into a C90 cassette at the end of my stiff arm. Not many interviews were in English, so questions and answers took twice the time. And translators had their own difficulties: understanding me was one, and understanding some of the thick local dialects in their own language was another. Often I had problems understanding my translators and sometimes, in playback, in understanding myself. Mercifully, I was spared technical breakdowns—the sturdy Sony only let me down one day up the Amazon when two interviews failed to record. The whole assignment was a challenge. Sometimes I wondered why I had ever got myself into it, but mainly it was fascinating—especially when listeners from diametrically different circumstances, from all over the world, began to say the same thing: they had met a Powerful Person who had thoroughly changed them.

Special mention must be made of the stories from FEBC and HCJB, who share the global task with Trans World Radio.

Providence could equally have brought me into contact with them first, but it didn't. Circumstances threw me in with Trans World Radio, and I limited my project to that network—which already encompassed the world. Taking on other Christian radio networks was just beyond me at the time, given my frail constitution (joke!), the size of my husband's pay packet, and time constraints. But the publishing process has a way of changing everything, and it became clear that FEBC and HCJB should be represented.

But by then I was back in New Zealand on a reduced pay packet and thousands of miles from anywhere. What do you do when manuscript deadlines are only seven weeks away and you have to go around the world again? You thank God for telephones and FAX machines, and you run up the largest six-week bill that your husband's ever faced. I managed to get twelve stories by these means, of varying quality, but the best I could do under the circumstances.

My very genuine apologies to FEBC and HCJB for underrepresenting you in relation to Trans World Radio—though your stories do show your impact. ELWA, I'm sorry, though I am sure your stories would match the best.

Just a few facts about FEBC and HCJB. HCJB was the first on the air, from Quito, Ecuador, and now broadcasts locally and internationally in twenty languages and thirty dialects from eleven short-wave transmitters for seventy-two hours each day. FEBC produced its first radio wave in 1948 and is now broadcasting in one hundred-six languages from five transmitting sites for more than 2,000 hours every week into all of Asia, the Middle East, Africa, and Latin America.

So altogether, by on-site interviews, letters, cassettes, telephone, and FAX I pulled out more than a hundred stories representing forty-eight different countries, twenty of which I personally visited. Of course, only a portion are presented here. My apologies to those many people who helped me but whose efforts are not represented here. I did write your stories; they just didn't make it.

A few other things. In some stories, names have been changed to protect people. Also, the stories are only as current as

the moment they were told to me; I simply don't know circumstances since. I have tried not to be too present in the telling but
to let the radio listeners speak for themselves. Please note that
the Roman Catholic church comes in for more than its fair share
of criticism—a simple reflection of the fact that I interviewed
more people influenced by Roman Catholicism than Protestant-
ism—because more of the world's Christian population is Roman
Catholic. Please remember that Vatican II (1962-1965) encouraged Bible reading by the faithful, that Pope John Paul II has
called for the re-evangelization of the church, and that spiritual
renewal is occurring.

The stories are glimpses into the lives of people who have
interacted with radio in some way. In some cases it has only
lightly touched them, as only one of a number of factors leading
to the Encounter. In other cases it has been the sole agent, and
the Encounter has been dramatic. If nothing else the stories
show an interesting range of impact. They were collected ran-
domly, in the sense that when you're wandering around with a
pack on your back, or dependent totally on what comes over the
wire, you can't be choosy.

The stories are human drama: people in predicaments we
all know about or can identify with in some way. They're being
honest with you, letting you into their lives, telling you what
went wrong and how it came right. They deserve to meet you.